D1359443

NEW YORK CITY STARWALKS

New York City
Starwalks

A Guide to the Exclusive Haunts, Habitats, and Havens of the Big Apple's Happening Celebs

By "The Star Sleuth"
LARRY "WOLFE" HORWITZ

ST. MARTIN'S PRESS / NEW YORK

NEW YORK CITY STARWALKS: A GUIDE TO THE EXCLUSIVE HAUNTS,
HABITATS, AND HAVENS OF THE BIG
APPLE'S HAPPENING CELEBS.

Design by Liney Li

Library of Congress Cataloging-in-Publication Data

Horwitz, Larry Wolfe.
New York City star walks / Larry Horwitz.
    p.   cm.
ISBN 0-312-09885-5
1. New York (N.Y.)—Guidebooks.
2. Walking—New York (N.Y.)—Guidebooks.
3. Celebrities—Homes and haunts—New York (N.Y.)
Guidebooks. I. Title.
F128.18.H66   1993
917.47'10443—dc20   93-8991
                    CIP

First Edition: August 1993

1 3 5 7 9 10 8 6 4 2

To

the *Starlight Foundation,*

an organization dedicated to

bringing magic to terminally ill children.

Their motto: Never say no.

CONTENTS

ACKNOWLEDGMENTS

I owe special thanks to several people who helped make it possible for me to complete this book.

Dana Joy, my wonderful wife, my inspiration, and an energetic researcher.

Jim Fitzgerald, an extraordinary editor, whose support and creative guidance was invaluable. His assistant, **Alex Kuczynski,** for her most spirited support.

Special thanks to editor **Robert Weil,** whose knowledge of Manhattan architecture is astonishing, and the rest of the staff at **St. Martin's Press,** whose warmth and attention goes unheralded in the publishing industry.

I'd like to express appreciation to my friend and cheerleader, talk-show host **Joe Franklin.**

A final round of applause goes to **Ed Lecaire, Michael Takiff, Mary Steele, Nancé Kaplan,** and the many other people who gave generously of their time.

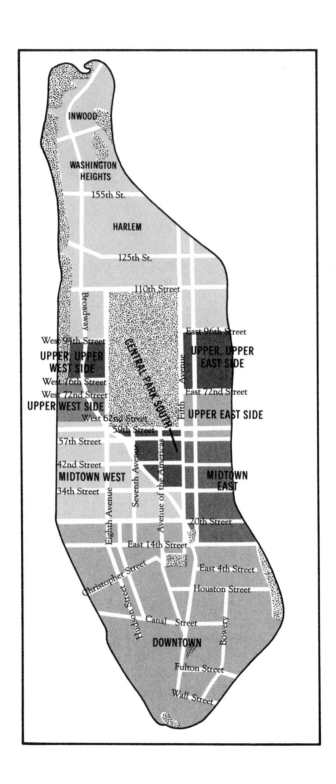

STAR ISLAND

☆ STARGAZER'S DELIGHT

Los Angeles may be Tinseltown . . . but New York City, the Big Apple, is the ultimate stargazer's heaven. What had been a long-kept secret, we may now declare with certainty: More stars make their home in Manhattan than in any other city in the world. Gotham is home not only to major movie stars but also to rock-and-roll greats, soap-opera personalities, superstar sports heroes, operatic divas and prima ballerinas, and even notorious criminal masterminds.

In fact, this tiny island off the East Coast of North America boasts more celebrities per square inch than any other town, district, state, or kingdom on the face of the globe. You may find it hard *not* to bump into world-class performers—dining in splendor at their favorite French restaurant or picking up coleslaw at the corner deli, trying on imported shoes at a trendy botique or buying socks from a street vendor, stepping out of a limousine or hopping onto a bus.

Movie stars like **Tom Cruise, Liza Minnelli, Bette Midler, Dustin Hoffman, Katharine Hepburn,** and **Michael J. Fox** are among the thousands of actors who are inspired and invigorated by residing in this city that never sleeps.

Rock and rollers flock to New York to catch the energy and excitement that emanates from life here. **Madonna, Billy Joel, Diana Ross, Mick Jagger,** and **Stevie Wonder** are among the stars who make music in soundproof studios just above the noisy streets.

It's not surprising that ballet stars such as **Mikhail Baryshnikov** and the late **Rudolf Nureyev** and opera favorites such as **Beverly Sills** and **Luciano Pavarotti** all have or have had homes within a small radius of Lincoln Center.

If you happen to be a news or talk-show aficionado, New York City is your mecca. **Barbara Walters, Peter Jennings,** and **Phil Donahue** are among the numerous personalities who live here.

Comedians often cite the bustling mosaic that is New York as inspiration for their best material. **Joan Rivers** tapes her television show in New York. **Rodney Dangerfield** owns a comedy club on the Upper East Side. **Woody Allen** makes his movies almost exclusively in Manhattan, and when he's hungry he visits the Carnegie Deli to eat pastrami with fellow funnymen like **Bill Cosby, Milton Berle,** and **Henny Youngman.**

Manhattan scores with sports celebrities, too. **Joe Namath, O. J. Simpson,** and **John McEnroe** are frequently spotted at the city's hottest restaurants. One popular hangout for athletes is **Mickey Mantle**'s Restaurant and Sports Bar, where the "Mick" himself is often on hand signing autographs.

Celebrities tend to cluster at certain restaurants. Often these eateries are owned by fellow entertainers. Others, like Sardi's and the Russian Tea Room, are New York landmarks that have been serving Manhattan's elite for years. Celebrities also frequent a select few ultraswank hair and beauty salons. Stars can be spotted at these establishments any day of the week.

A majority of celebrities residing in Manhattan prefer to live in areas bordering Central Park. Some stars opt for the serenity and sophistication of the Upper East Side. Many radiate toward the artsy Upper West Side. Still others prefer to project a chic downtown persona and therefore reside in the cutting-edge neighborhoods of Greenwich Village and Tribeca.

☆ STAR TREKKING

Some of your favorite stars are a dodgy lot. **Brooke Shields** enters a 57th Street movie theater just before the credits roll, sits in the back row, and retreats as the final line is spoken. Sunglasses and a kerchief do little to conceal **Sophia Loren** as she shops the pricey 5th Avenue boutiques close to home. **Katharine Hepburn** promenades through town in slacks, her chin held high, as befits the independence of spirit for which this Hollywood legend is renowned. **Al Pacino** enjoys disguising himself as pal **Dustin Hoffman** as he watches roller skaters in Central Park. **David Letterman** dons shades for his stroll down Canal Street, wishing he could duplicate the chameleonlike skills of neighbor **Robert De Niro,** known to take extreme measures to recreate his body for a particular film. (Just about the only technique Robert hasn't used in his character preparation is plastic surgery—not yet, anyway!)

Other celebrities, however, enjoy the commotion and adoration that come from fan recognition. **Madonna** loves teasing hordes of admirers with her escapades as she roves about town. Bar and restaurant owners **Patrick Swayze, Bruce Willis, Arnold Schwarzenegger,** and **Matt Dillon** consider their fame critical to building the clientele of their respective establishments. **Michael J. Fox** and **Bill Cosby** bend over backward to accommodate their throngs of loyal fans.

As in any exact science, there are rules to follow when one hopes to spot a favorite celebrity. Always be alert and aware, since some of your most awe-inspiring discoveries will happen when least expected. Stars clothe themselves at the same stores we browse in and they buy food at our neighborhood grocers. Their dogs do not walk themselves, but, like ours, they pull on a leash attached to a human hand. And when a child needs to be taken to a piano lesson, the youngster musn't be kept waiting, even if Mommy or Daddy has to interrupt that phone call about a multipicture deal.

If a face appears familiar but is dismissed as an imposter because of a hat, mustache, scarf, or glasses, you've probably been too hasty in your judgment. I'll never forget the time **Bob Hope** told me emphatically that I was mistaken, he wasn't the celebrated comedian-actor-golfer. I found that the jokester had put one over on me when moments later the man holding open the limousine door said, "Good morning, Mr. Hope." **Cher** is one of many performers who dress in clothes one would never expect to see on so flamboyant a star. She enjoys Manhattan because here one can dress down without fear of disapproval. Seeing **Christie Brinkley** with her glowing face unobstructed one day and covered in dark glasses and kerchief the next can create havoc for stargazers.

Frequenting the places your favorite stars are known to fancy can turn chance into probability. If you know that a particular celebrity enjoys being seen in a certain Gotham eatery, by all means make a reservation. If the star owns the restaurant, he or she is even more likely to be there. Hairdressing salons are also wonderful for spotting all kinds of celebrities. For a few extra dollars, why not get those bangs trimmed at a salon that caters to your favorite performers? Charity events and Broadway openings are also perfect stargazing occasions. Hoping to be noticed, the rich and famous do themselves up and turn on the charm.

Just remember that celebrities, like yourself, need their privacy. Never disturb them while they enjoy a meal, converse with a friend, or relax at home. If the opportunity to meet them arises, tell them how much you enjoy their work. Be courteous. The courtesy they show in return may surprise you.

☆ THE STAR SLEUTH

Madonna jogging through Central Park lacking make-up and having her hair bundled up under a baseball cap cleverly screening those trademark features, **Joan Rivers** walking dog **Spike** down Madison Avenue, **Michael Douglas** and **Dustin Hoffman** lunching in adjoining booths at the Russian Tea Room, **Brooke Shields** munching popcorn at a local cinema—these are but a few of my celebrity sightings during just the last several months.

Whether I am uptown or down, indoors or out, whether it's day or night, a celebrity often appears. A number of sightings have occurred near areas cordoned off to accommodate film crews. New York can seem like a film studio's back lot, with the multitude of features, commercials, rock videos, and television shows being shot all over town.

I am puzzled that so many journalists portray New York as a city where no people in their right mind would ever reside. That view obviously is not held by the thousands of major celebrities who call Gotham home.

In researching the whereabouts of stars' homes, as well as their favorite restaurants, hairstylists, and health clubs, creative methods were called for. Long talks with doormen, waiters, beauticians, dry cleaners, butchers, and elevator operators were important. Horse-drawn carriage drivers and chatty cabbies were excellent sources of information.

After double- and triple-checking such sources, I realized that a trip to the city's Bureau of Records would be worthwhile. Long hours of verifying ownership reports proved most valuable.

I discovered more than one thousand homes of celebrities in Manhattan. My conclusion was that New York City is *the* home of stars. This island is where the rich and famous began their careers and where they have come to reap the benefits now that they've reached their goals.

Aside from the obvious enjoyment this information has given New Yorkers and visiting tourists, many other positive effects have resulted. Geography teachers have reported that celebrity addresses helped them teach their students about Manhattan's districting: Students identify favorite actors with areas of residence (**Madonna**—Upper West Side; **De Niro**—downtown, etc.). Charities have used the data for important causes and fund-raising efforts. Stars contacted by the Starlight Foundation, for example, a nonprofit organization that grants wishes to sick children, have given generously of their time and money. **Michael J. Fox** and **Kurt Vonnegut** were more than happy to draw doodles for auction by the New Dramatists at the Russian Tea Room.

Whether you hope to catch glimpses of particular stars or just learn more about their lifestyles, your best bet is to begin your quest by taking the walking tour of their neighborhood included in this book.

Get those feet moving. Keep your eyes open. Watch the stars shine.

T O U R 1

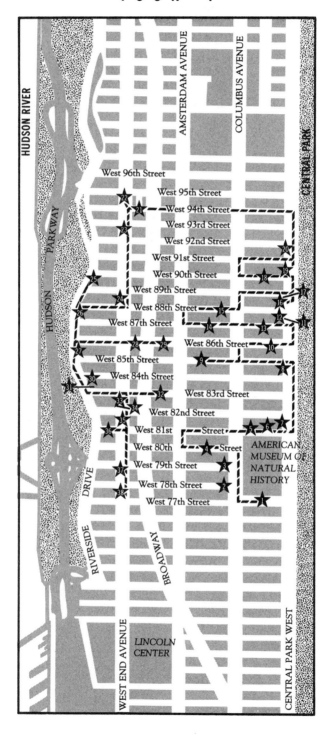

SUPERSTARS
UPPER UPPER WEST SIDE

T O P ⭐10 T E N

STARS IN THE AREA

Kevin Bacon ☆ Robert Duvall ☆ Michael J. Fox ☆ Mick Jagger ☆ Tatum O'Neal ☆ Tony Randall ☆ Arnold Schwarzenegger ☆ Beverly Sills ☆ Meryl Streep ☆ Barbra Streisand

NUMBER	ADDRESS	NAME
1	6 West 77th Street	**Peter Allen** (deceased) **Nancy Friday** *Bonfire of the Vanities*
2	100 West 78th Street	**Christopher Reeve**
3	101 West 79th Street	**Boy George** **Billy Jean King** **Cleo Laine**
4	118 West 80th Street	**Christopher Walken**
5	15 West 81st Street	**Liv Ullmann**
6	11 West 81st Street	**Teri Garr** **Nastassia Kinski**
7	211 Central Park West	**Tatum O'Neal** **John McEnroe** **Peter Jennings** **Diane Sawyer** **Mike Nichols** **Helen Gurley Brown** **Isaac Stern** **Beverly Sills** **Tony Randall** **Phyllis Newman** **Adolph Green** **Rock Hudson** (deceased) **Meyer Lansky** (deceased) **Margaret Mead** (deceased)
8	241 Central Park West	**Richard Dreyfuss**
9	123 West 85th Street	**Howard Rollins**
10	10 West 86th Street	**Christine Lahti**
11	271 Central Park West	**Meryl Streep** **Mark Hamill** **Jane Pauley** **Garry Trudeau** **Laurence Luckinbill** **Lucie Arnaz**

12	275 Central Park West	**Arnold Schwarzenegger** **Maria Shriver**
13	27 West 87th Street	**Linda Lavin**
14	176 West 87th Street	**Jackee Harry**
15	113 West 88th Street	**Earl "the Pearl" Monroe**
16	279 Central Park West	**Yasmin Khan** **Miles Davis** (deceased)
17	285 Central Park West	**Ed Bradley** **Joyce Randolph**
18	55 West 90th Street	**Barbara Hershey**
19	300 Central Park West	**Michael J. Fox** **Tracy Pollan** **Faye Dunaway** **Garrison Keillor** **Tuesday Weld** **Pinchas Zuckerman**
20	320 Central Park West	**Barbra Streisand** **Dianne Wiest** **Swoosie Kurtz**
21	250 West 94th Street	**Barnard Hughes**
22	710 West End Avenue	**Ronnie Spector**
23	666 West End Avenue	**Charles Grodin**
24	585 West End Avenue	**Raul Julia**
25	173 Riverside Drive	**Diahann Carroll** **Vic Damone**
26	155 Riverside Drive	**Margaux Hemingway**
27	137 Riverside Drive	**Kevin Bacon** **Kyra Sedgwick**
28	257 West 86th Street	**Robert Duvall**
29	225 West 86th Street	**Isaac Bashevis Singer** (deceased)
30	118 Riverside Drive	**Anne Meara** **Jerry Stiller**
31	110 Riverside Drive	**Babe Ruth** (deceased)
32	225 West 83rd Street	**Harvey Fierstein**
33	470 West End Avenue	**Penny Marshall**
34	465 West End Avenue	**Barbara Barrie**
35	440 West End Avenue	**Jill Clayburgh**
36	304 West 81st Street	**Mick Jagger**
37	390 West End Avenue	*Network* *Eyewitness* *Heartburn*
38	365 West End Avenue	**Tony LoBianco**

This trendy area between 75th and 96th streets attracts a broad range of famous entertainers, intellectuals, and arty eccentrics. **Barbra Streisand, Mick Jagger,** and **Beverly Sills** are examples of the varied creative luminaries who populate the Upper, Upper West Side.

This tour will take you through a hodgepodge of architectural delights, beginning with the beautifully designed building that was the former home of **Peter Allen** and ending with the residence of **Tony LoBianco**.

Since residents are noticeably more relaxed and friendly than in most other parts of town, the celebrities you might pass on the tour will probably reflect that attitude. Remember always to be friendly and courteous, and never disturb a star at his or her home or in a restaurant.

A diversity of interesting-looking residents in a setting of extraordinary buildings makes this a perfect location for feature films and television shows. Scenes for NBC's "Law and Order" are frequently shot close to the Hudson River. And just about every street near the American Museum of Natural History has been used in a major film. Such movies include *The Fisher King,* starring **Robin Williams; Neil Simon's** *Chapter Two;* and *The Pick-up Artist,* with **Molly Ringwald.**

The area to be covered on this tour is bounded by West 75th Street on the south, West 96th Street on the north, Central Park West on the east, and Riverside Drive on the west.

Starting Address:	**Central Park West and 77th Street**
Length of Tour:	**2 Hours, 35 Minutes**
Best Starting Time:	**10:00 A.M. or 2:00 P.M.**
Subway:	**A, B, C, or D to 81st Street**
Bus:	**7, 10, 11, or 79**
Bring Along:	**Canteen, breath mints, and trendy clothing**

☆ THE TOUR

Our journey begins a few doors away from Central Park West, on 77th Street. From the subway stop at Central Park West and 81st Street, head south down Central Park West. Make a right on 77th Street. On your left will be our starting point.

Peter Allen's residence up until his death in 1992, 6 West 77th Street⊕ is a fitting place to start our tour because, though an owner of homes in both the Big Apple and Los Angeles, the singer-songwriter admitted only to being a New Yorker. Described by **Tom Wolfe** in his best-selling novel *Bonfire of the Vanities* as the most beautiful in town, this block is just across Central Park from the home of Peter's ex-wife, **Liza Minnelli**—the high-energy couple split up in 1974. A consummate showman, Peter performed with the Rockettes at Radio City Music Hall, starred in a Central Park concert, and wrote the music for a Broadway musical. Another resident of 6 West 77th Street is writer **Nancy Friday,** chronicler of the intimate secrets of women and men.

Now look across the street at the American Museum of Natural History, a heterogeneous group of buildings occupying a four-block area formerly called Manhattan Square and fronting on Central Park West between 77th and 81st streets. The original portion of this massive structure was built in the Romanesque Revival style. After you've checked out the immense dinosaur skeletons, plan a visit to the museum's Hayden Planetarium, where stars of New York are often found gazing at stars of outer space in one of the planetarium's entertaining presentations, which combine music and a laser light show.

Back on Earth, many hot celebrities go for the burn at the Equinox Fitness Club, 342 Amsterdam Avenue. Mornings are best for stargazers hoping to glimpse some of their favorite actors, including **Steve Martin** and **Melanie Griffith.** The club is easily reached by walking one and a half blocks west to Amsterdam Avenue, turning left, and proceeding a few doors south on the west side of the road.

... **W**..
hile weekday mornings are indeed prime time for spotting famous faces at the Equinox, stargazers should approach the iron-pumping celebrities with caution. **Steve Martin** *in particular is known to be grumpy before he has his morning coffee.*

....

Walk a block south on Amsterdam Avenue, turn right on 75th Street, walk a block to Broadway, and just off the southeast corner is a hip, laid-back club that has long attracted celebrities from all areas of the entertainment industry: the China Club, 2130 Broadway. Monday night is a sure bet for spotting such megastars as **Mick Jagger, Carly Simon, Billy Joel, Kathleen Turner,** and even the "Material Girl"

China Club, 2130 Broadway

herself, **Madonna.** You might even catch one of them treating the crowd to an impromptu performance, as happened recently when **Kathleen Turner** sang a duet with her husband, bandleader **Jay Weiss.**

*... he doorman at the China Club remembers one Monday evening when **Eddie Murphy** parked his limo in front of the night spot and tossed $4,000 in cash to the homeless. A vivid memory still lingers of smiling beggars hopping into taxis, dining on delicacies, and exchanging their $100 bills for the finest liquor.*

Christopher Reeve

It's a bird, it's a plane—no, it's **Christopher Reeve** (otherwise known as Superman). This Gotham-born actor's career was launched into orbit when he played the title role in *Superman* (1978). He doesn't live in a phone booth but has a lovely home at 100 West 78th Street.② Three blocks north on Broadway, a right on 78th Street, and two blocks to Columbus Avenue will put you on Christopher's doorstep. To head directly from Peter Allen's former home to Mr. Reeve's residence complex, a short walk west on 77th Street and one block north on Columbus Avenue is the route to take.

One block north on Columbus Avenue, at 101 West 79th Street③ is a building with a fascinating mix of celebrity occupants. One spacious pad belongs to flamboyant vocalist **Boy George,** whose outrageous theatrics have made him one of the most successful British rock stars to hit the States. This singer-songwriter is a perfect fit, especially when in costume, for the freethinking spirit New York's West Siders are known to possess. Other residents of this prestigious building include outspoken tennis pioneer **Billie Jean King** and singer-actress **Cleo Laine,** known for her role in *The Mystery of Edwin Drood* on Broadway.

A block further north and a few doors left of Columbus, at 118 West 80th Street④ lives actor **Christopher Walken,** a native New Yorker known for his exceptional work in dozens of movies, including *The Deer Hunter* (1978). Since Christopher has also appeared in over a hundred plays, he appreciates his home's proximity to New York's Theater District.

Brunch at Sarabeth's Kitchen, 423 Amsterdam Avenue, (212-496-6280) reminds one of waking up in a Vermont country inn. Enjoy the aroma of freshly baked bread and pastries as you dine on homemade delicacies. A major lunching spot for actors, models, and soap stars, this cozy eatery is a stargazer's paradise. The restaurant is on Amsterdam Avenue, only a few doors west of our present location.

We now walk to 81st Street, turn right, and head two blocks east toward Central Park. Great dramatic actress and natural beauty **Liv Ullmann** has a luxury apartment at 15 West 81st Street. ⑤ Born in Tokyo, but of Norwegian descent, Liv spent part of her childhood in Gotham and returned to New York in later years to star in many Broadway hits. Nominated for two Academy Awards, Liv is also active in UNICEF and other major charities.

··· **O**··
ne afternoon, **Liv Ullmann** *tore down a New York street in hot pursuit of screen legend* **Greta Garbo.** *Liv was hoping to discuss her role in* Anna Christie, *one which her fellow Swede had made famous decades before. Unfortunately, Garbo the Great got away, so we'll never know whether she was following her credo, "I vant to be alone," or if she had simply seen Liv's performance and wasn't impressed.*

··

Liv's next-door neighbor, at 11 West 81st Street, ⑥ is actress **Teri Garr.** Teri established herself as a leading film comedienne in 1982 when she starred opposite fellow West Sider **Dustin Hoffman** in the New York–made film *Tootsie.* In the same building lives delicately sensuous film star **Nastassia Kinski.** Nastassia's notoriety dates back to her 1981 nude poster, photographed by **Richard Avedon,** in which she appeared intertwined with a sprawling python.

Our next stop is the Beresford, 211 Central Park West, ⑦ the corner of 81st Street. Known for its striking architecture, this corner complex is massive yet elegant. Its three picturesque towers overlooking Central Park provide a romantic setting for the building's many celebrity tenants.

Beresford, 211 Central Park West

Actress and director **Tatum O'Neal** and her husband, tennis ace **John McEnroe,** have a spacious home in the Beresford. Married on Long Island, New York, in August of 1986, the star couple has three children. This storybook romance has taken on tough times with Tatum's decision to pursue her acting career despite her husband's objections. Although a champion around the globe, John saves his most outstanding tennis for New York's own U.S. Open, where he's won four championships.

ABC's "World News Tonight" anchorman **Peter Jennings,** his wife, **Kati,** and their two children also have their home in the Beresford. Peter's prior Big Apple residence, which he shared with ex-wife, Valerie, was a couple of blocks south at 135 Central Park West.

Peter is as likely to share an elevator with **Diane Sawyer** at the office as he is at home. This fellow ABC journalist, cohost of "Prime Time Live," lives in the Beresford with her husband, **Mike Nichols,** the film and stage director who's earned six Tony Awards. He's won an Oscar, too—for his direction of *The Graduate*, the 1967 film that introduced the world to **Dustin Hoffman.**

... **P**...
eter Jennings seemed at ease as he signed for deliveries and checked tenants' IDs while sitting in the Beresford's lobby during the summer of 1991. The anchorman had turned doorman-for-a-day because the regular workers were on strike.
....

Also residing in one of the Beresford's three illuminated towers are author-publisher **Helen Gurley Brown** and her New York–born husband, filmmaker **David Brown.** Helen's best-selling book, *Sex and the Single Girl* was the launching pad she used to take over and revitalize *Cosmopolitan* magazine.

Violinist **Isaac Stern,** who plays some two hundred concerts a year, has an elegantly furnished home in the same building, as does another legendary musician, Brooklyn–born opera star **Beverly Sills,** known as "Bubbles" to friends and fans.

Yet one more show-biz resident of the Beresford is **Tony Randall.** Tony, who moved to New York at age nineteen to study acting with **Sanford Meisner,** is best known for his role as the obsessive Felix Unger on the hit comedy series "The Odd Couple." Actress **Phyllis Newman** and her husband, New York–born lyricist **Adolph Green,** are another celebrity couple in the star-studded building.

Rock Hudson had a six-room home in the Beresford until his death in 1985. Shortly after his death, a number of his belongings were taken from the residence and sold for charity at a New York auction house. Underworld boss **Meyer Lansky** and anthropologist **Margaret Mead** also had homes in the Beresford. Meyer was a resident through the 1940s while Margaret lived there until her death in 1978.

This area's unique character has made it a location site for many film and television productions. *The Pick-up Artist* (1987), starring **Molly Ringwald,** was set in the vicinity of the Museum of Natural History. The horses in the **Robin Williams** movie *The Fisher King* (1991) came down 81st Street between Columbus and Amsterdam avenues. In **Neil Simon's** *Chapter Two* (1979), **James Caan** had his home on 76th Street between Central Park West and Columbus Avenue. TV's "The

Equalizer" and "The Hard Way" were filmed at the Beacon Theater, 2142 Broadway, as well as on neighborhood streets; and on West End Avenue, **Paul Sorvino** is contantly seen acting in scenes for "Law and Order." Many of these location sites lie along the route of this tour.

Our next stop is the residence of energetic and likable Brooklyn–born actor **Richard Dreyfuss,** who resides three blocks north along the park at 241 Central Park West. ⑧ Richard won an Academy Award for Best Actor in *The Goodbye Girl* (1977). Shot in Gotham, the film costarred Richard's fellow West Sider **Marsha Mason.**

We now head a block north to 85th Street, turn left, and proceed just past Columbus Avenue to our next residence. At 123 West 85th Street⑨ is the home of actor **Howard Rollins.** His neighbor, at 10 West 86th Street⑩ is actress **Christine Lahti,** who received an Academy Award nomination for her supporting role in the 1984 film *Swing Shift.* She resides one block north and one block toward Central Park from Mr. Rollins.

··· **C**··
    hristine Lahti *abandoned her maiden N.Y. City acting job because she lacked proper tolerance for the freezing cold and snow. Working as a mime in Central Park only a few feet from her present home, Christine decided that indoor employment was more to her liking. She felt a white painted face that turned red would not be convincing to her customers.*
··

Meryl Streep

Around the corner and a block north along the park resides delicately beautiful leading lady of American stage and screen **Meryl Streep.** Her home is at 271 Central Park West. ⑪ Born across the river in New Jersey, Meryl originally moved to the Big Apple with the hope of becoming an opera singer, and for a time she studied with **Beverly Sills**'s voice teacher. In the same building resides actor **Mark Hamill,** known for his role as Luke Skywalker, the boyish hero of the *Star Wars* trilogy.

Television reporter **Jane Pauley** and her husband, **Garry Trudeau,** creator of the "Doonesbury" comic strip, also have their home at 271 Central Park West. Other residents of this classic building include actor **Laurence Luckinbill** and actress **Lucie Arnaz,** daughter of television stars **Lucille Ball** and **Desi Arnaz.**

Seven-time Mr. Olympia and America's top box-office attraction **Arnold Schwarzenegger** lives a few doors north at 275 Central Park West[12] with his wife, **Maria Shriver.** He married the attractive newscaster, a niece of the late **President John F. Kennedy,** in 1986.

Arnold Schwarzenegger

If you're a major star and you miss your mom's apple strudel, buy a restaurant and have a gourmet chef prepare it using her recipe. I'm not saying that's why **Arnold Schwarzenegger** opened his new restaurant, Planet Hollywood, so close to home, but his mother **Aurelia**'s apple strudel is on the menu.

Actress **Linda Lavin,** best recognized for her long stint in the starring role of the CBS television sitcom "Alice," resides at 27 West 87th Street,[13] just off Central Park West. About a block west, at 176 West 87th Street,[14] is comedic actress **Jackee Harry.**

Continue on 87th Street west to Amsterdam Avenue. This might be a perfect time to stop for a light meal or just to freshen up. Popover Cafe at 551 Amsterdam Avenue (212-595-8555) has a fun menu, including the puffy bread called the popover, as well as egg dishes such as a horseradish omelet and a strawberry butter that whets the taste buds of stars like **Kim Basinger** and boyfriend, **Alec Baldwin.** If you'd rather get some takeout food and keep moving, visit Barney Greengrass, at 541

Amsterdam Avenue, (212-724-4707) on the same block. The regular customers of this seafood lover's emporium include **Shelly Winters, Alec Baldwin, Peter Max,** and **George Burns.**

Next, head north to 88th Street, turn right, and walk east. One hundred thirteen West 88th Street⑮ is the home of former New York Knickerbocker **Earl "the Pearl" Monroe,** one of the flashiest players in basketball history. If you see Earl driving up to his town house in a Rolls-Royce, he might be returning from one of his frequent meetings with troubled youth.

If you have extra time, you might enjoy a five-to-ten-minute stroll—north one block along Columbus Avenue and west one block on 89th Street—to the neighborhood horse stable! The Claremont Riding Academy, at its unlikely 175 West 89th Street location, is always prepared to rent mounts to such celebrities as **Diana Ross, Jacqueline Onassis,** and **William Hurt** for leisurely trots through Central Park. In the 1981 movie *Eyewitness,* William Hurt opened the gates of this hundred-year-old landmark, allowing the horses to roam free and help him overpower a murderer.

Meanwhile, back at the ranch—anyway, east along 89th Street to Central Park West, then south one block to 279 Central Park West⑯—we have the home of **Yasmin Khan,** daughter of actress **Rita Hayworth** and **Prince Aly Khan.** In the same building lived jazz trumpeter **Miles Davis** until his death in 1991. One of music's true innovators, the legendary jazzman's influence will be felt by generations of jazz artists to come.

Backtracking a block along Central Park, we come to a classically designed building at 285 Central Park West,⑰ home of broadcast journalist **Ed Bradley** of "60 Minutes." Ed, whose spacious home is decorated with art and photos from his work and travels in Asia, takes full advantage of neighborhood eating establishments and works out at a local health club six days a week.

Two hundred eighty-five Central Park West is also home to actress **Joyce Randolph.** Joyce is remembered as Trixie Norton, wife to **Art Carney's** Ed, in "The Honeymooners," **Jackie Gleason's** popular television series of the fifties.

Walk two blocks north to 90th Street and stroll west. Fifty-five West 90th Street⑱ is where sensuously beautiful actress **Barbara Hershey** has her residence.

Carmine's 2450 Broadway, (212-362-2200) is a popular, inexpensive family-style restaurant with a Little Italy atmosphere that you might want to partake of one evening. The only drawback is the usual hour-long wait for a table. Even stars like **Kevin Bacon** have been too hungry to wait. The restaurant is reached by directing yourself west on 90th Street a couple of blocks, making a right on Broadway, and heading a few doors north.

Kevin might have skipped the wait at Carmine's to head up the street to another favorite restaurant. At 2452 Broadway, the Pumpkin Eater (212-877-0132) features healthy, naturally prepared foods. One waitress gloats about serving **Alec Baldwin,** who tipped her a $100 bill for no other reason than that he liked her.

We now return to Central Park West and one of the hottest buildings in town. The Eldorado, 300 Central Park West,[19] attracts the most famous of stars with its beautiful twin towers and richly decorated lobby. The Art Deco structure was used by writer **Herman Wouk** as the fictional residence of his heroine Marjorie Morningstar. East to Central Park West and south a short distance will place you at the Eldorado.

Superstar of television and film, **Michael J. Fox** is one of the many celebrity inhabitants of the Eldorado. Actively involved in a number of New York charities, Michael recently made an unusual donation to the New Dramatists (an organization devoted to assisting up-and-coming playwrights): a very snappy "doodle" that was auctioned off at the Russian Tea Room. Ironically, Michael's real-life wife is radiant actress **Tracy Pollan,** who played his girlfriend on the hit television serial "Family Ties."

Michael J. Fox

... **M**ichael J. Fox *hasn't let his fame hide his friendly nature. Recently spotted in front of his Central Park West residence, loading his automobile with bundles of diapers, the superstar treated onlookers to a smile and a few soft-spoken words.*

Faye Dunaway

The Eldorado is also home to lovely leading lady **Faye Dunaway.** Faye, whose career was launched in 1962 when she joined the Lincoln Center Repertory Company, has starred in such blockbusters as *Bonnie and Clyde* (1967), *Chinatown* (1974), and *Network* (1976). In the same building resides writer and radio host **Garrison Keillor.**

Another blond actress who lives at the Eldorado is **Tuesday Weld,** a native New Yorker typecast as a sex kitten in many of her film and TV roles. Also living in the building is violinist and conductor **Pinchas Zuckerman.** This virtuoso is regarded as one of the finest musicians of our time.

Superstar of stage, screen, and recording, Brooklyn–born **Barbra Streisand** resides at 320 Central Park West[20] only a couple of blocks farther north. Barbra worked in Manhattan as a switchboard operator and then as a theater usher before winning a Greenwich Village nightclub contest. Soon after that victory, she appeared in *I Can Get It for You Wholesale,* the 1962 musical revue in which she played opposite her husband-to-be (and *ex*-husband-to-be), **Elliott Gould.** She then starred as Fanny Brice in the sensational 1964 Broadway musical hit *Funny Girl.* Finally, in 1970, she was presented with a special Tony Award as Actress of the Decade. A few years back, Barbra tried to move crosstown to 1021 Park Avenue but was rejected by the building's board of directors. Seems the stodgy East Siders wanted to avoid the spotlight that follows this top celebrity everywhere she goes.

··· **W**·······································
······ hen *a superstar calls for emergency medical assistance,*
the problem may be critical. Recently, **Barbra Streisand** *could
not return to the set of* The Prince of Tides *until her favorite
manicurist rushed to the star's home to repair her sickly fingernail.*
···

Barbra's neighbors in this luxurious building at 320 Central
Park West include actresses **Dianne Wiest,** best known for the
neurotic characters she plays in many Woody Allen films, and
Swoosie Kurtz, winner of two Tony Awards.

Our journey now takes us west toward the scenic Hudson
River. Head two blocks north to 94th Street, turn left, and
walk three blocks. The last street you cross should be Broadway. If your feet need a rest, take the 96th Street crosstown
bus; otherwise, a brisk fifteen-minute walk will bring you to
the home of an outstanding character actor, New York–born
Barnard Hughes, at 250 West 94th Street. ㉑

Walk west to the end of the block and make a right, and
you come to 710 West End Avenue, ㉒ where you'll find the
residence of **Ronnie Spector,** lead singer in the 1960s rock-
and-roll band the Ronnettes. Sarcastically witty actor **Charles
Grodin,** who learned his craft from **Lee Strasberg** and **Uta
Hagen,** lives a couple blocks south at 666 West End
Avenue. ㉓ Continue south to find the home of Broadway
and film star **Raul Julia,** who resides at 585 West End
Avenue. ㉔

Farther west, keep an eye out for **Diahann Carroll.** This
actress and singer, who began her career performing at New
York nightclubs while studying sociology at New York University, resides at 173 Riverside Drive㉕ with her husband,
singer **Vic Damone.** Their home is reached by walking one
block west on 88th Street, turning right, and heading north
two blocks.

Two blocks south brings you to actress and model **Margaux
Hemingway,** labeled the "Face of a Generation" after appearing on the covers of *Vogue* and *Time* magazines, who has
her home at 155 Riverside Drive. ㉖ Another two blocks
down, at 137 Riverside Drive㉗ in a luxurious yet discreet
location, is the home of handsome young film star **Kevin Bacon**
and his sweet, comely blond-haired wife **Kyra Sedgwick.**

A brisk five-minute walk east on 86th Street brings you to
257 West 86th Street, ㉘ home of **Robert Duvall,** a remarkable
actor known for the intricate detail he pours into every characterization. His neighbor a few doors east, at 225 West 86th

Street,[29] was Nobel laureate **Isaac Bashevis Singer,** who died in 1991. This great writer, who spent the last thirty years of his life as an integral part of the West Side community, was a frequent patron of neighborhood restaurants, where he would order only vegetarian meals.

Heading back west along 86th Street, we turn left on Riverside Drive. Two blocks down, we come to the home of husband-and-wife comedy team **Anne Meara** and **Jerry Stiller.** They have an attractive home in a luxurious building at 118 Riverside Drive[30] overlooking the Hudson. Continuing south, we arrive at 110 Riverside Drive,[31] where legendary New York Yankee **Babe Ruth** had an eleven-room home he shared with his wife, **Claire Hodgson Ruth,** until his death in 1948. Walk two blocks east, along 83rd Street, to 225 West 83rd Street,[32] the residence of Tony Award–winning actor-playwright **Harvey Fierstein.** We next retrace our steps west on 83rd Street to West End Avenue, where we turn left and walk a few doors down.

Actress and director **Penny Marshall** spent her early years tap-dancing in her mother's New York dance school. Penny, who costarred in the hit TV show "Laverne and Shirley," has her home at 470 West End Avenue.[33] Nearby, at 465 West End Avenue,[34] is the home of movie and stage actress **Barbara Barrie.**

Continue south a block to the home of actress **Jill Clayburgh,** the daughter of prominent Manhattanites, who ironically was nominated for an Academy Award for her characterization of a wealthy, intelligent, emotionally overwrought New Yorker in the 1978 movie *An Unmarried Woman.* An avid jogger, Jill and her Reeboks can often be spotted close to her home at 440 West End Avenue.[35]

Mick Jagger

Round the corner of 81st Street to see the home of one of rock and roll's greatest performers, **Mick Jagger** of the Rolling Stones. Mick owns an elegant town house at 304 West 81st Street. ㊱

Don't be shocked if you see **Mick Jagger** and **Jerry Hall** on the Central Park bridle path. Mick and his glamorous wife enjoy Manhattan's finest pleasures, including horseback riding, clubs, and lots of shows. Most of his friends in town are ordinary nine-to-fivers.

Back on West End Avenue, walk two blocks farther south to the Apthorp, 390 West End Avenue, ㊲ a grand limestone apartment house built for William Waldorf Astor in 1906. Constructed around a courtyard and fountain, and entered only through bronze gates, the complex was used in the 1976 movie *Network* as a rendezvous site for **Faye Dunaway** and **William Holden,** as **Signourney Weaver's** home in the 1981 movie *Eyewitness* and as **Meryl Streep** and **Jack Nicholson's** residence in *Heartburn* (1986).

Continuing south another block to 365 West End Avenue, ㊳ you find the home of actor **Tony LoBianco.**

Barbra Streisand

If you're ready to head home, why not stop at Zabar's at 2245 Broadway? To reach this location, head east on 77th Street to Broadway, turn left, and walk north three blocks. There you'll be able to choose from a feast of prepared foods and an array of smoked meats and cheeses. **Lauren Bacall** and **Kathleen Turner** are among the many celebrities who shop at this gourmet landmark. When filming in town, **Woody Allen** hires Zabar's to cater meals for his cast and crew.

ZABAR'S®

···**B**···
arbra Streisand brought a bag of goodies from Zabar's to her son and his coach, **Nick Nolte,** *who were both worn out from an afternoon of football practice in Central Park. Although the snack was fictional—the scene appeared in* The Prince of Tides—*it was familiar to the high-powered actress–director: Her home in the 1991 film was, as is her real home, located just minutes away from her favorite spot for takeout dining.*
··

The tour ends on the corner of Broadway and 80th Street. Check out some of the other diverse shops along this busy thoroughfare. Otherwise, the bus service along Broadway is quite frequent. If you'd prefer the subway, walk one block south to 79th Street and Broadway to catch the 1 or the 9.

TOUR 2

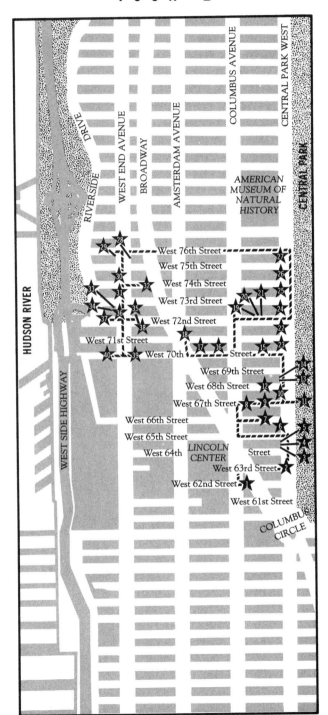

STAR WALK
UPPER WEST SIDE

T O P ⭐ T E N
STARS IN THE AREA

Lauren Bacall ☆ Michael Douglas ☆ Mia Farrow ☆ Dustin Hoffman ☆ Madonna ☆ Steve Martin ☆ Marsha Mason ☆ Paul Simon ☆ Sting ☆ Bruce Willis

NUMBER	ADDRESS	NAME
1	61 West 62nd	**Jacqueline Bisset** **Alexander Godunov**
2	25 Central Park West	**Alexis Smith** (deceased) **Ethel Merman** (deceased)
3	1 West 64th Street	**Madonna** **Melanie Griffith** **Don Johnson** **Ed Asner** **Carol Kane**
4	41 Central Park West	**Gwen Verdon**
5	50 Central Park West	*Three Men and a Baby*
6	55 Central Park West	*Ghostbusters* **Marsha Mason** **Calvin Klein**
7	10 West 66th Street	**Isaac Asimov** (deceased)
8	45 West 67th Street	**Phoebe Cates** **Kevin Kline**
9	1 West 67th Street	**Leroy Neiman** **Richard Thomas** **Joel Grey** **Noel Coward** (deceased) **Norman Rockwell** (deceased) **Rudolph Valentino** (deceased) *My Dinner with Andre* *The Money Pit*
10	75 Central Park West	**Carroll O'Connor** **Jimmy Breslin**
11	Tavern on the Green	*Only When I Laugh* *Ghostbusters* *Heartburn*
12	19 West 68th Street	**James Dean** (deceased)
13	80 Central Park West	**Gloria DeHaven**

14	88 Central Park West	**Paul Simon** Sting **Celeste Holm** **Joan Copeland**
15	15 West 70th Street	**Maureen Stapleton**
16	135 West 70th Street	**Candace Early**
17	155 West 70th Street	**Jonathan Frakes** **Jeannie Francis**
18	171 West 71st Street	**Daryl Hannah**
19	27 West 72nd Street	**Tiny Tim** **Martin Balsam**
20	15 West 72nd Street	**Shelley Winters** **Farley Granger**
21	12 West 72nd Street	**Sigourney Weaver**
22	115 Central Park West	**Fred Astaire** (deceased) **George S. Kaufman** (deceased) **Isadora Duncan** (deceased) **Frank Costello** (deceased) **Meyer Lansky** (deceased) **Lucky Luciano** (deceased) **Milton Berle** **Zero Mostel** (deceased)
23	101 Central Park West	**Jack Weston** **Dorothy Loudon**
24	1 West 72rd Street	**Lauren Bacall** **Roberta Flack** **Rudolf Nureyev** (deceased) **Connie Chung** **Maury Povich** **John Madden** **John Lennon** (deceased) **Yoko Ono** **Sean Lennon** **Rex Reed** **Leonard Bernstein** (deceased) **Judy Holliday** (deceased) **Boris Karloff** (deceased) **Rosemary Clooney** *Rosemary's Baby* *House of Strangers*
25	135 Central Park West	**Carly Simon** **Mia Farrow** **James Levine** **Susan Strasberg** **Lee Strasberg** (deceased)
26	145–146 Central Park West	**Bruce Willis** **Demi Moore** **Dustin Hoffman** **Diane Keaton** **Elaine May** **Keir Dullea** **Mary Tyler Moore**

		Barry Manilow Mick Jones Billy Squire Victoria Tennant Steve Martin Rita Hayworth (deceased) Jack Dempsey (deceased) Harold Arlen (deceased)
27	151 Central Park West	Michael Douglas Diandra Douglas Basil Rathbone (deceased)
28	333 West End Avenue	James Taylor
29	336 West End Avenue	Larry Storch
30	300 West End Avenue	Harry Belafonte
31	290 West End Avenue	Christopher Columbus
32	2109 Broadway	Igor Stravinsky (deceased) Florenz Ziegfeld (deceased) Enrico Caruso (deceased) *Three Days of the Condor*
33	277 West End Avenue	Bernadette Peters
34	270 West End Avenue	Paul Sorvino Marlon Brando
35	266 West End Avenue	Mae West (deceased)
36	263 West End Avenue	James Earl Jones Judith Rossner
37	330 West 72nd Street	Lori Singer
38	254 West 72nd Street	Ashford and Simpson
39	271 West 70th Street	Tama Janowitz
40	315 West 70th Street	Cicely Tyson

The Upper West Side, stretching roughly from West 61st to West 76th Street, is the single-most-star-studded area in Manhattan. Within this neighborhood is an area I have labeled Star Walk, a ten-block strip along Central Park West that contains the greatest concentration of movie stars and other celebrities anywhere in the world. This tour begins with **Jacqueline Bissett's** residence and culminates with the home of the stunning actress **Cicely Tyson.**

Lincoln Center for the Performing Arts is a focal point of the area. For the stars, it's a short walk to this world-renowned arts complex, which stages ballets, operas, and concerts, as well as theatrical productions and film festivals. Lincoln Center has been used as a backdrop in many films, including *The Turning Point* (1977), starring **Anne Bancroft** as a prima ballerina, **Mel Brooks's** *The Producers* (1968), in which **Gene Wilder** and **Zero Mostel** danced with joy around the center's impressive fountain, **Cher** and **Nicholas Cage** in the delightful

comedy *Moonstruck* (1987), and the 1984 box-office blockbuster *Ghostbusters.*

ABC television studios inhabit huge chunks of Upper West
Side real estate. Many entertainers refer to these ABC prop-
erties as the "campus," an appropriate term, since numerous
stars reside in the classic buildings clustered around these
broadcast facilities.

The area we will be covering on this tour is bounded by
West 61st Street on the south, West 76th Street on the north,
Central Park West on the east, and Riverside Drive on the
west.

Starting Address:	**Broadway and 62nd Street**
Length of Tour:	**1 Hour, 50 Minutes**
Best Starting Time:	**10:00 A.M. or 2:00 P.M.**
Subway:	**A, B, C, D, 1, or 9 to Colum-bus Circle**
Bus:	**5, 7, 10, or 104**
Bring Along:	**Pencil and paper, lunch money, opera glasses, and camera**

☆ THE TOUR

We begin our tour only a few doors west of Broadway on 62nd
Street. The Broadway bus takes you to within only a few yards
of the corner of 62nd Street. From the Columbus Circle subway
stop at Broadway and 59th Street, head north on Broadway,
past the New York Colliseum on your left, for three blocks.
Make a left onto 62nd Street and on the north side of the
street is our starting point.

A luxurious building at 61 West 62nd Street① is home to
beautiful actress **Jacqueline Bisset** and her partner, **Alexander
Godunov,** the stunning Russian ballet star. Jacqueline had an
early longing to become a ballet dancer herself but gave it up
because she was too tall.

Since you're around the corner from Lincoln Center, why
not check out what's playing in this all-in-one cultural mecca?
Lincoln Center for the Performing Arts stretches along Broadway between 62nd and 66th streets. If you enjoy the dancing

of **Mikhail Baryshnikov,** the singing of **Luciano Pavarotti,** or the acting of any number of stars, then this spot is for you! In the summertime, you might stop for a drink at one of the outdoor cafés that surround a magnificent fountain in the very center of Lincoln Center Plaza. Gaze past the fountain and you'll notice two murals suspended just inside the Metropolitan Opera House. These paintings are the work of the late Russian-born artist Marc Chagall.

Heading east toward Central Park along 63rd Street and making a right on Central Park West, we come to the Century building, 25 Central Park West,② which replaced the ill-fated Century Theater in 1931. The Century is the former residence of actress **Alexis Smith** (born **Gladys Smith**) who died at the age of seventy-two on June 9, 1993. This huge Art Deco structure was also at one time home to the full-throated singer-actress **Ethel Merman.** One block north on Central Park West, we arrive at our next destination.

Madonna, who resides at 1 West 64th Street③ is not only the neighborhood's most famous star, she's also one of the most frequently spotted. O'Neals (212-787-4663), owned by actor **Patrick O'Neal** a few doors west at 49 West 64th Street, is known to be one of her favorite restaurants. Stargazers mention regular sightings of the singer jogging or riding her bicycle home from Central Park. Although one of the world's highest-paid entertainers, the "Material Girl" saved a penny or two when her residence was recently remodeled: She hired her designer brother to do the job.

Madonna

B... *efore she moved into her present digs,* **Madonna** *tried to purchase a home in the San Remo (145 Central Park West) in 1985 for $1.4 million. Her offer was refused, however, because the building's board wanted to dodge potential problems stemming from her fame and notoriety. (The star had recently been featured in revealing* Playboy *and* Penthouse *layouts and the publicity was intense.) Interestingly enough, actress* **Diane Keaton** *was the only board member to insist on the singer's acceptance.*

1 W. 64th Street

Recently, sexy New York–born actress **Melanie Griffith** and her husband, movie and television star **Don Johnson,** took up residence in **Madonna's** 1 West 64th Street building. In the same complex resides **Ed Asner,** long featured as the grumpy but lovable Lou Grant on "The Mary Tyler Moore Show," and the talented actress **Carol Kane.** Their neighbor in the same building, although with a different street address, 41 Central Park West, ④ is Tony Award–winning Broadway hoofer **Gwen Verdon.**

Major motion pictures are constantly being filmed in and around the buildings along Central Park West. **Ted Danson, Steve Guttenberg,** and **Tom Selleck** shared a penthouse at 50 Central Park West⑤ in the 1987 movie *Three Men and a Baby.* Next door, at 55 Central Park West, ⑥ **Sigourney Weaver** found spooks in her kitchen in *Ghostbusters,* the 1984 blockbuster. Actress **Marsha Mason (Neil Simon's** ex) and fashion designer **Calvin Klein** both reside in that very same, very spirited building. Our next stop is a short walk west on 65th Street from Central Park West.

Sfuzzi, 58 West 65th Street, (212-873-3700) is one of the trendy Italian restaurants in the area that attract stars like **Billy Joel, Robin Williams,** and **Arnold Schwarzenegger.** This bistro is a good choice if you plan a cultural evening at Lincoln Center.

SFUZZI

In the area surrounding West 66th Street and Columbus Avenue, you will find ABC television studios, where shows such as "All My Children," "One Life to Live," "Loving," "Ryan's Hope," "Live with Regis and Kathie Lee," "20/20," "Good Morning America," and "World News Tonight" are produced. (See Chapter Eleven for information on how you can obtain free tickets to attend some of these shows.)

Isaac Asimov, the famed science-fiction writer, had his home across from ABC Studios at 10 West 66th Street, ⑦ between Columbus Avenue and Central Park West, until his death in April of 1992. A block west on 66th to Columbus

Avenue, a right, and another right takes you to 45 West 67th Street, ⑧ the residence of celebrity couple **Phoebe Cates** and **Kevin Kline.**

··· **W**hen Shakespearean actor *Kevin Kline fell in love, the real-life Romeo packed up his belongings and moved into the home of his Juliet, actress **Phoebe Cates.** I Love You to Death was the name of the 1990 film in which Kevin appeared, not one of the marriage vows he exchanged with Phoebe during their 1989 wedding.*

Located a few doors east on the same block at 1 West 67th Street⑨ is the Hotel des Artistes, a beautiful New York landmark originally intended to house sculptors and painters. This elaborate building with its double-height windows and carved stone figures covering the exterior is still home to at least one painter, **Leroy Nieman,** who is well known for his colorful depictions of sports heroes.

Another inhabitant of the Hotel des Artistes is New York–born actor **Richard Thomas,** best known for his Emmy Award–winning portrayal of John-Boy in the television series "The Waltons." His parents, **Richard** and **Barbara Thomas,** once owned the prestigious New York School of Ballet. Richard's neighbor in the building is the versatile **Joel Grey,** famed as the evil master of ceremonies in Broadway and film versions of the musical *Cabaret,* for which he won both Tony and Oscar.

Former residents of this classic hotel include **Noel Coward, Norman Rockwell,** and **Rudolph Valentino.**

··· **R**udolph Valentino *rented a bachelor pad at Hotel des Artistes in 1922. The silent-screen heartthrob was married at the time, but his wife **Jean Acker,** was living in California.*

The restaurant Café des Artistes (212-877-3500) takes up much of the hotel's ground floor. This romantic dining spot is enhanced by its huge murals, the work of artist **Howard**

Chandler Christy, depicting naked romping nymphs. This New York City institution was featured in the 1981 movie *My Dinner with Andre* and the 1986 comic farce *The Money Pit.*

Our next stop takes us east to 67th Street and Central Park West. When New York–born actor **Carroll O'Connor** played Archie Bunker in the television sitcom "All in the Family," he may have had to ignore some of the lessons he taught his students when he was an English teacher in the city's public schools. Carroll resides at 75 Central Park West[10] in the same building as gritty New York newspaper columnist **Jimmy Breslin.**

TAVERN ON THE GREEN

Looking east, just inside Central Park, across from 67th Street, is a magically designed restaurant in a spectacular setting. Tavern on the Green[11] (212-873-3200) has been seen in many films, including *Only When I Laugh* (1981), *Ghostbusters* (1984), and *Heartburn* (1986). Stars the world over consider this fantasy of lights a must-see on visits to Gotham.

Walk north one block on Central Park West, turn left, and a few doors down on 68th Street is our next location. **James Dean,** the movie star who symbolized his era, never relinquished the twelve-foot-square New York apartment he acquired early in his career. This "rebel without a cause" returned to this 19 West 68th Street[12] home in 1955, a few months before his fatal auto accident.

James Dean, 19 W. 68th Street

Retrace your steps back along 68th Street to 80 Central Park West,[13] the home of stage and screen actress **Gloria DeHaven.** With the decline of the screen musicals in the fifties, Gloria switched to the New York stage and more dramatic roles.

Continuing north, two of the world's most successful musicians live in a luxury limestone high rise at 88 Central Park West.[14] Although the music of **Paul Simon** is very different from that of **Sting,** both of these rock-and-roll superstars seem inspired by intellectually conceived notions and a desire to do good deeds.

Also residing at 88 Central Park West is New York–born actress **Celeste Holm,** who had to walk only a few doors down to 50 Central Park West for her appearance in the 1987 film *Three Men and a Baby.* **Joan Copeland,** another veteran of stage and screen, lives at 88 Central Park West, as well.

Next, we walk north on Central Park West to 70th Street and turn left. A few doors down, in a four-story walk-up at 15 West 70th Street,⑮ resides the very talented actress **Maureen Stapleton.** Maureen moved to Gotham in the 1940s, when she was a waitress by day and an acting student by night. Continue along 70th Street, heading west to reach the homes of some of television's most popular performers.

Since several TV soap operas are taped in the area, many soap stars reside here, too. Among them is **Candace Early,** who lives in a stunning building, restored in 1928, at 135 West 70th Street.⑯ Her neighbors a few doors west at 155 West 70th Street,⑰ are actor **Jonathan Frakes** and his soap-star wife, **Jeannie Francis.** One block north, the corner of 71st Street and Broadway, takes us to our next destination.

Sexy film star **Daryl Hannah** has made a big splash with handsome prosecuting attorney **John F. Kennedy, Jr.** Their romantic adventures are the frequent subject of New York tabloids. Daryl's home in the very sculptured twelve-story Dorilton complex, built in 1902, at 171 West 71st Street⑱ is an ideal spot to find solitude from a hectic schedule of both studying film at New York University and preparing for an upcoming movie role.

Cafe Luxembourg (212-873-7411), 200 West 70th Street, has a charming and cozy at-

CAFE
LUXEMBOURG

mosphere that attracts actors such as **Tom Cruise** and **Kevin Kline.** A meal at this pricey bistro might be a fun adventure to begin a special evening. Walk back to 70th Street, turn right, and just past Amsterdam Avenue will put you at the entrance.

Actors **Christian Slater, Gary Oldman, Annabella Sciorra Gary Busey** and basketball coach **Pat Riley** prefer the casual setting and the huge pasta portions offered at *Columbus Trattoria* (212-799-8090) 201 Columbus Avenue. The restaurant is also a hangout for many N.Y. Ranger hockey players including **Brian Leetch, Mark Messier** and **Mike Richter. Mikhail Baryshnikov, Robert De Niro** and **Regis Philbin** had ownership of this bustling neighborhood eatery up until the end of 1992. The restaurant is located on the corner of 69th Street and Columbus Avenue and can be reached from Cafe Luxembourg by walking east on 70th Street two blocks and south a block on Columbus Avenue.

... **I**f your dream is to marry a movie star, pull up a chair at Columbus Trattoria. That's what **Vanessa Sorvino** did. Actually, actor **Paul** had invited her friend over to his table, but when Vanessa tagged along, he knew he'd found the woman who would bring "law and order" to his life.

Need rest and refreshment? I suggest heading two blocks north on Columbus Avenue and stopping at the ice cream parlor and eatery to which actress **Mia Farrow** takes her children when they deserve a sweet treat. Diane's, 249 Columbus Avenue, is known not only for its frosty delights but also for its excellent hamburgers.

Continue north one block to 72nd Street, turn right, and halfway down the block is our next stop. On 72nd Street, with its unusual mix of commercial and residential buildings, resides naïve comic singer **Tiny Tim** in a high-rise hotel with a friendly staff. Tiny lives at 27 West 72nd Street,[19] as does Oscar and Tony Award–winning actor **Martin Balsam.**

A few doors east, at 15 West 72nd Street,[20] is the lavish home of colorful actress **Shelley Winters,** who learned her craft in New York at the Actors Studio. Another film star in the building is **Farley Granger.**

Tall and beautiful leading lady **Sigourney Weaver** lives in a luxurious building across the street at 12 West 72nd Street.[21] This accomplished native New Yorker is the daughter of a British actress and a former president of NBC.

Sigourney Weaver

... **O**nly in Gotham can a star be on the job after just a brisk ten-minute walk. In the movie Ghostbusters (1984), **Sigourney Weaver** had only to stroll over to 55 Central Park West to film that humorous scene in which she finds a monster in her refrigerator.

Straight ahead on 72nd, at the southwest corner of Central Park West, we come upon one of the most elegant and prestigious apartment houses in New York City, the Majestic, 115 Central Park West.[22] The edifice was built on the site of the old Hotel Majestic, a prominent resort in the early 1900s and the residence of such notables as **Fred Astaire, George S. Kaufman,** and dancer **Isadora Duncan.** Rebuilt in 1931, the Majestic has been home to some celebrities not known for their frendliness: Underworld chieftains **Frank Costello, Meyer Lansky,** and **Lucky Luciano** all had mammoth apartments here. More likely to make you smile comedic greats **Milton Berle** and **Zero Mostel,** also had residences in the building for many years.

Backtrack a short distance south on Central Park West to the home of actor **Jack Weston** at 101 Central Park West.[23] Jack supported himself in New York as a dishwasher and elevator operator before his career gained momentum. His neighbor in the building is actress **Dorothy Loudon.** We next backtrack north on Central Park West to the northwest corner of 72nd Street.

The Dakota, 1 W. 72nd Street

The Dakota, 1 West 72nd Street,[24] may well be New York's top celebrity address. Their attraction to the German Renaissance–style building overlooking Central Park can easily be explained with one glance at its châteaulike design.

Completed in 1884 from plans by **Henry Hardenbergh,** who also designed the Plaza Hotel, this stately structure was so isolated that New Yorkers joked that it might as well be out in the Dakotas. Designed to accommodate any number of servants, the building boasts a large wine cellar and huge residences with fourteen-foot ceilings.

Countless luminaries from all areas of the entertainment industry have been tenants on the Dakota's roster. The list includes rock-and-roll stars, leading actors and acresses, and a world-renowned composer.

Beautiful New York–born actress **Lauren Bacall,** once dubbed "The Look" by a studio publicity department, has long lived in the Dakota. Lauren has been a vivid figure on the Gotham scene, beginning with her early years at the American Academy of Dramatic Arts, then as a cover-girl model, followed by her emergence as a screen goddess, and culminating with a Broadway run that won her a Tony.

Another Dakota resident is one of the nation's top vocalists, Grammy Award–winner **Roberta Flack.** Her former neighbor in the building was one of the most celebrated ballet dancers of our time, **Rudolf Nureyev.** Rudolf, who was perhaps the greatest male dancer since Vaslav Nijinsky, died of cardiac complications resulting from AIDS in January of 1993 at the age of 54.

News anchor **Connie Chung** and her polished talk-show host husband, **Maury Povich,** have a luxurious home in the Dakota, as does former pro football coach and television sports commentator **John Madden.**

The Dakota is still home to **Yoko Ono,** widow of the deceased Beatle **John Lennon.** In honor of her slain husband, who was shot and killed at the building's entrance in the fall of 1980, Yoko donated funds for Strawberry Fields, a peaceful garden across the street in Central Park. Their son, singer-songwriter **Sean Lennon,** lives at the Dakota, as well.

It's easy to understand why film critic and celebrity interviewer **Rex Reed** chose the Dakota as his home. It's convenient to have a decade's worth of interviews within a three-block radius.

Other luminaries who have resided in the Dakota have included **Leonard Bernstein, Judy Holliday, Boris Karloff,** and **Rosemary Clooney.**

Ms. Clooney was definitely not, however, the subject of *Rosemary's Baby.* The 1968 film boosted the building's notoriety and piqued the public's curiosity concerning the Dakota. *House of Strangers* (1949) starring Edward G. Robinson featured the landmark complex in an earlier feature film. The book *Life at the Dakota,* by Stephen Birmingham (Random House, 1979), brought to light more tales involving the residents. Photographers, both amateur and professional, are constantly lurking around the building, scouting for a favorite star or just enjoying its classic setting. A constant parade of limousines flows through the iron gates that adorn the 72nd Street entrance.

Continue north along the park one block to the Langham, 135 Central Park West.㉕ This building's lobby is ornately decorated with marble and bronze and with crystal chandeliers. In 1905, when the structure was erected, the four suites per block-long floor each rented for over $4,000 per year. Today's residents, who must have to shell out a much larger sum, include singer-songwriter **Carly Simon.** Carly is presently writing children's books under the auspices of her editor, East Sider **Jacqueline Onassis.**

Mia Farrow

Also living in the Langham is the delicately beautiful actress **Mia Farrow,** who until most recently was often spotted with ex-boyfriend **Woody Allen** and her children, strolling leisurely through Central Park. Woody used Mia's Langham residence in his 1986 film *Hanna and Her Sisters,* in which Mia starred.

The Langham, 135 Central Park West

··· **M**ia Farrow *lives with her many natural and adopted children (including Satchel, her child with* **Woody Allen***) at 135 Central Park West, while ex-boyfriend Woody lives across the park. Ironically enough,* **Diane Keaton,** *Woody's ex-girlfriend (and ex–leading lady), resides next door to Mia.*

Conductor and pianist **James Levine** also has his spacious home in the Langham, as does New York–born actress **Susan Strasberg.** Surprisingly, Susan never attended the Actors Studio, the legendary dramatic training ground headed by her father, **Lee Strasberg.** Lee had an elegant home in the Langham until his death in 1982.

We now head north a block to one of the most star-studded buildings in Gotham. Major entertainers flock to the San Remo, a massive twin-towered complex at 145–146 Central Park West.㉖

Movie-star couple **Bruce Willis** and **Demi Moore** recently purchased a $10 million home in the San Remo. The location is perfect because it's within walking distance of Bruce's new restaurant, Planet Hollywood, at 140 West 57th Street. Bruce has lived the American dream, rising from his humble New York beginnings as a bartender at the Kamikaze nightclub to his present lifestyle as a wealthy, happily married superstar and father.

The San Remo

Dustin Hoffman is another actor who started at the bottom, washing dishes, checking coats, and selling toys at Macy's during his rise to stardom. Now able to afford a luxury residence at the San Remo, this remarkable acting genius enjoys jogging through Central Park or lunching at the Russian Tea Room, 150 West 57th Street.

Demi Moore

Dustin Hoffman *is a favorite among doormen in the San Remo. This generous actor regularly takes them along when he attends major sporting events.*

Academy Award–winning actress **Diane Keaton,** who studied her profession in New York with **Sanford Meisner,** has her home in the San Remo. Another resident at this prestigious address is talented actress, screenwriter, and director **Elaine May.** Actor **Keir Dullea** and Brooklyn-born television and movie star **Mary Tyler Moore** also live here.

... **M**ary Tyler Moore *called upon celebrity pet groomer* **Lee Day,** *who came to her home and sang to her dog,* **Dash,** *while shampooing the pampered puppy's coiffure. The event was enlivened when Dash shot Mary in the face with soap while the actress was accompanying Lee in a popular show tune.*

Another San Remo inhabitant is singer-composer **Barry Manilow.** Fellow resident musicians include rock guitarist **Mick Jones** and rhythm-and-blues soloist **Billy Squire.**

Most of the celebrities in the San Remo choose to live in the 145 Central Park West tower, but some home buyers have been bucking the trend. One such couple is **Victoria Tennant** and her "wild and crazy" husband, **Steve Martin,** who occupy a home at 146 Central Park West in the Sam Remo's second tower.

Steve Martin

... **S**teve Martin *and wife,* **Victoria Tennant,** *are slowly expanding their territory in the exclusive San Remo. In Manhattan, the only way to increase the size of your home is to convince your neighbors to move. Steve and Victoria have purchased the residence next to theirs and will soon combine the two units.*

Past residents of the San Remo have included **Rita Hayworth,** the legendary screen star of the 1940s, and **Jack Dempsey,** the world-champion prizefighter. Songwriter **Harold Arlen** also called the San Remo home until his death in 1986. Just up the street, at 151 Central Park West, [27] is the Kenilworth, where superstar **Michael Douglas** lives with his wife, **Diandra.** Their early-nineteenth-century Russian furnishings, working fireplaces, and dazzling view of Central Park make for a very

comfortable home. This imposing prewar architectural mas-
terpiece was also the residence of **Basil Rathbone,** otherwise
known as the cunning Sherlock Holmes.

The Kenilworth, 151 Central Park West

Michael Douglas

Area *residents recall spotting Frankenstein (**Boris Karloff**)
and Sherlock Holmes (**Basil Rathbone**) strolling side by side
through Central Park. The two actors were close friends and lived
near each other.*

A brisk ten-minute walk toward the Hudson River—two dollars by taxi, if your feet are sore—brings you to the home of
singer **James Taylor** at 333 West End Avenue.[28] If you choose
to walk, your best bet is to head one block north on Central
Park West, turn left onto 76th Street, and go four blocks west
to West End Avenue; turn left there, and a few doors south
is Taylor's residence. His neighbor across the street, at 336
West End Avenue,[29] is **Larry Storch,** who starred in the
sixties sitcom "F-Troop."

Continue south a few blocks to the residence of New York–
born actor and calypso vocalist **Harry Belafonte,** who has an
attractive home at 300 West End Avenue.[30] Director **Christopher Columbus,** discovered by America in the hit comedy
family movie *Home Alone,* resides a few buildings south at 290
West End Avenue.[31] Head east one block on 74th Street to
the corner of Broadway to arrive at our next location.

The Ansonia, 2109 Broadway,[32] is a stunning building
built in the style of hotels on the French Riviera. The building's thick soundproof walls have made it a favorite of musical
figures like composer **Igor Stravinsky,** impresario **Florenz Zieg-
feld,** and tenor **Enrico Caruso.** The structure also houses the
American Musical and Dramatic Academy. (If you need to
use a pay phone, the Ansonia has a few of them, too—just
stop in the lobby.) The Ansonia was featured in the engrossing

1975 mystery film *Three Days of the Condor,* in which **Robert Redford** flees for his life from the building's back exit. We now walk west back to West End Avenue, turn left, and stroll one block south to our next stop.

The Ansonia
2109 Broadway

At 277 West End Avenue,③ we come upon the residence of New York–born actress **Bernadette Peters,** who has been a stage and screen success since the age of five. Bernadette's neighbor is actor **Paul Sorvino,** also a New York native. Paul lives across the Street at 270 West End Avenue,③ where **Marlon Brando** lived while acting on Broadway early in his remarkable career.

... **I**f you'd like to *"come up and see me some time,"* you're late: buxom bombshell **Mae West,** who resided at 266 West End Avenue,③ passed away in 1980.

Continuing south, distinguished Tony Award–winning actor **James Earl Jones** has his home at 263 West End Avenue,③ as does best-selling author **Judith Rossner.**

The excitement of busy 72nd Street attracts performers such as actress **Lori Singer,** who resides at 330 West 72nd Street.③ Her home can be reached by turning right onto 72nd Street from West End Avenue. Lori's neighbors are the soul-singing duo **Ashford and Simpson,** who live east one block at 254 West 72nd Street.③ We continue again down West End Avenue and make a left on 70th Street.

Author **Tama Janowitz,** who lives with her two Yorkshire terriers at 271 West 70th Street,③ helps to continue the tradition of the Upper West Side as a literary center. A few doors west resides talented **Cicely Tyson,** at 315 West 70th Street.④ Cicely, once married to jazz great **Miles Davis,** co-founded the Dance Theatre of Harlem in hope of giving something back to the community in which she was raised.

Walk one long block east on 70th Street to Broadway to find bus transportation north and south. Turn left, and two blocks north on Broadway will bring you to the 1, 2, 3, or 9 subway trains.

TOUR 3

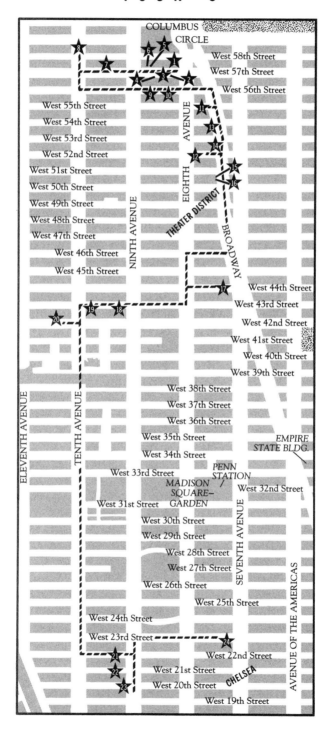

COLUMBUS CIRCLE
West 58th Street
West 57th Street
West 56th Street
West 55th Street
West 54th Street
West 53rd Street
West 52nd Street
West 51st Street
West 50th Street
West 49th Street
West 48th Street
West 47th Street
West 46th Street
West 45th Street
West 44th Street
West 43rd Street
West 42nd Street
West 41st Street
West 40th Street
West 39th Street
West 38th Street
West 37th Street
West 36th Street
West 35th Street
West 34th Street
West 33rd Street
West 32nd Street
West 31st Street
West 30th Street
West 29th Street
West 28th Street
West 27th Street
West 26th Street
West 25th Street
West 24th Street
West 23rd Street
West 22nd Street
West 21st Street
West 20th Street
West 19th Street

EIGHTH AVENUE
NINTH AVENUE
TENTH AVENUE
ELEVENTH AVENUE
SEVENTH AVENUE
AVENUE OF THE AMERICAS
BROADWAY

THEATER DISTRICT
EMPIRE STATE BLDG.
PENN STATION
MADISON SQUARE-GARDEN
CHELSEA

REGARDS TO BROADWAY
MIDTOWN WEST

T O P ★ T E N
STARS IN THE AREA

Gene Hackman ☆ Angela Lansbury ☆ Maureen McGovern ☆
Virginia Mayo ☆ Al Pacino ☆ Jane Powell ☆ Nipsey Russell
☆ Jack Warden ☆ Irene Worth ☆ Steve Van Zandt

NUMBER	ADDRESS	NAME
1	301 West 57th Street	**Gene Hackman** **Al Pacino** **Eileen Fulton**
2	322 West 57th Street	**Steve Van Zandt**
3	340 West 57th Street	**Virginia Mayo** **Hal Holbrook**
4	350 West 57th Street	**Christopher Hewett** **Georgia Engel** **Arthur Tracy**
5	347 West 57th Street	**Greg Gumbel**
6	353 West 57th Street	**Nipsey Russell**
7	435 West 57th Street	**Will Jordan**
8	899 10th Avenue	*Fame* *Up the Down Staircase*
9	353 West 56th Street	**Melvin Van Peebles**
10	333 West 56th Street	**Irene Worth** **Dee Hoty** **Carole Shelley**
11	230 West 55th Street	**Jane Powell**
12	250 West 52nd Street	Neil Simon Theater
13	1697 Broadway	Ed Sullivan Theater
14	1681 Broadway	Broadway Theater
15	1634 Broadway	Winter Garden
16	1633 Broadway	Gershwin Theater
17	234 West 44th Street	*Switch*
18	400 West 43rd Street	**Jack Warden**
19	484 West 43rd Street	**Angela Lansbury** **Eric Douglas**
20	529 West 42nd Street	**Maureen McGovern**
21	435 West 22nd Street	**Rip Torn**

22	467 West 21st Street	**Anthony Perkins** (deceased)
23	434 West 20th Street	**Blair Brown**
24	222 West 23rd Street	**Mark Twain** (deceased)
		Dylan Thomas (deceased)
		Bob Dylan
		Sid Vicious (deceased)
		Arthur Miller
		Eugene O'Neill (deceased)
		William Burroughs
		Arthur Clarke

Central Park Place
301 W. 57th Street

Starring in a major motion picture can make an actor rich and famous . . . but Broadway is where legends are made. Performers know that critics rarely rave about an actor's skill and versatility unless that star has shown competence night after night in front of a live audience. Recently, movie stars, television actors, and pop-music performers have taken to the Broadway stage in droves. Singing sensation **Debbie Gibson,** who debuted January 7, 1992, in the long-running Broadway production of *Les Misérables,* dreamed of this opportunity to prove herself as an actress. The twenty-one-year-old young singer dispelled her teenybopper image when she brought the house down with an incredible performance.

Al Pacino, Angela Lansbury, Irene Worth, and **Gene Hackman** number among the many stars who reside in and around the Theater District. There is an excitement, an electricity, that these talented performers enjoy just by being on the scene. Even stars who haven't performed on a stage for years anxiously await their next chance to walk those few block onto a Broadway stage and into immortality.

The final leg of our journey takes us to the colorful neighborhood of Chelsea. Celebrities hoping to enjoy a relaxed and quiet environment, where town houses and loft buildings are the rule, buy into this richly ethnic area.

Our tour begins at 301 West 57th Street, home to **Al Pacino** and **Gene Hackman,** and culminates at the legendary Chelsea Hotel, 222 West 23rd Street. The area covered is bounded on the east by Broadway and on the west by the Hudson River; 57th Street is the northern boundary, and 20th Street is the southernmost point.

Starting Address:	**57th Street and 8th Avenue**
Length of Tour:	**1 Hour, 45 Minutes**
Best Starting Time:	**11:00 A.M., 1:00 P.M., or 6:00 P.M.**
Subway:	**A, B, C, D, 1, or 9 to Columbus Circle**
Bus:	**10, 30, 57, 58, or 104**
Bring Along:	**Camera, money for fake watch, and *New York Times* theater listings**

☆ THE TOUR

Columbus Circle, with its merging traffic from a myriad of directions, is two blocks north of our starting point at 57th Street and 8th Avenue. As you head south on 8th Avenue, to your back will be **Gaetano Russo's** monument to Christopher Columbus, erected in 1892 and marking the very center of the circle.

Our tour commences at the home of New York–born superstar **Al Pacino**—Michael Corleone to fans of the *Godfather* saga. This two-time Tony Award–winning actor resides in Central Park Place, an ultramodern high rise at 301 West 57th Street, ① corner of 8th Avenue. An alumnus of **Herbert Berghof's** New York acting school, Al saved up money for tuition by work-

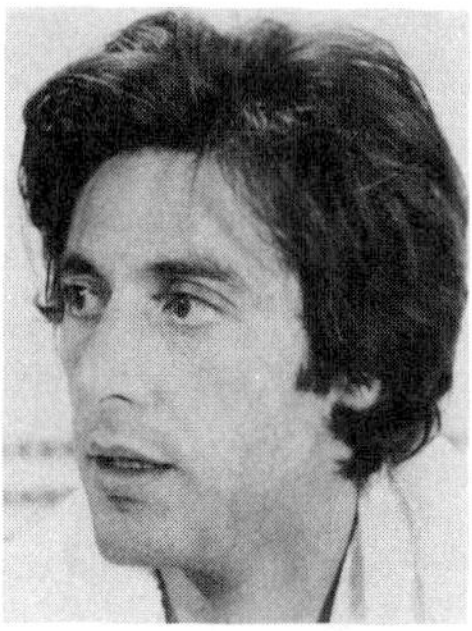

Al Pacino

ing at menial occupations (usher, porter, delivery boy). No doubt he also cut expenses by eating at his uncle's pizzeria on upper Broadway. Al is known to be a very private person, so much so that columnist **Earl Wilson** once labeled him "the male **Greta Garbo.**"

... **D**isguised in glasses and wearing a fake mustache, **Al Pacino** enjoyed the experience of anonymously blending in at a concert in New York. When asked what his disguise was, he responded, half-smiling, that he was impersonating **Dustin Hoffman.**

Gene Hackman

Another former movie usher residing in Central Park Place is **Gene Hackman,** respected among his peers as an actor's actor for his versatility and professionalism. Gene's superb talent earned him an Oscar for his performance as New York detective Popeye Doyle in the 1971 film *The French Connection.* The building is home as well to soap-opera star **Eileen Fulton.**

Across the busy thoroughfare, in the brown-bricked Sheffield, lives rock-and-roll star **Steve Van Zandt.** The wide driveway in front accommodates the steady flow of limousines pulling up to this 322 West 57th Street address.②

Down the block is the Parc Vendome, a group of four separate buildings on both 56th and 57th streets. To find out why this complex is packed with celebrities, take a peek at the lovely open garden at the rear of each building. This beautifully landscaped archi-

Parc Vendome

tectural gem, with its white Roman columns and picturesque concrete fountain, is truly breathtaking.

The Parc Vendome's 340 West 57th Street③ address is

home to glamorous blond actress **Virginia Mayo,** leading lady to comedians **Danny Kaye** and **Bob Hope** in films of the forties and fifties. Another resident is stage, television, and film actor **Hal Holbrook,** whose stardom began with his one-man show, *Mark Twain Tonight!*

Three fifty West 57th Street④ is the second 57th Street entrance of this fashionable establishment. One resident who must appreciate the building's beige canopies is actor **Christopher Hewett,** remembered best for his portrayal of the very tidy Mr. Belvedere on the popular television sitcom of the same name. Christopher spends his free time collecting Staffordshire china, but he has nearly exhausted his home's available space with his extensive assortment.

Kooky actress **Georgia Engel,** whose big break came on "The Mary Tyler Moore Show," also lives at 350 West 57th Street. Another resident is the "Street Singer," **Arthur Tracy,** whose romantic hit song "Marta" sold over 18 million records.

Back across the street, at 347 West 57th Street,⑤ resides sportscaster **Greg Gumbel.** The Colonnade, as this attractive building is named, has a bowling alley–sized lobby filled with an eclectic collection of art.

At 353 West 57th Street,⑥ in the Henry Hudson Hotel, lives comedian **Nipsey Russell,** whose forte is clever rhymes. Since his appearance in the 1978 film *The Wiz,* Nipsey has kept a somewhat low profile.

Comedian and actor **Will Jordan** has his home in a white brick building at 435 West 57th Street,⑦ just past 9th Avenue. His impressions of celebrities such as **Ed Sullivan** and **Humphrey Bogart** remain the standard by which younger mimics are judged.

A pleasant morning or evening makes for excellent stargazing, since celebrities enjoy a leisurely stroll to work. Many popular performers spend their day at the CBS Television Broadcast Center, a massive complex of buildings located at 518 and 524 West 57th Street and taking up much of the south side of the block between 10th and 11th avenues. Studio audiences line up early in the mornings to sit in on shows, including "The Joan Rivers Show" and "Geraldo." "60 Minutes," "The CBS Evening News," and "As The World Turns" are also taped in the Broadcast Center's studios.

On the north side of this same block is Unitel Studios, located at 515 West 57th Street. "The Sally Jessy Raphael Show" is taped here at 11:00 A.M. Monday through Thursday before a live audience. Other shows are produced here as well, including "Sesame Street," the long-running children's favorite.

Do you wonder where aspiring young high school students dreamed of stardom in the 1980 movie *Fame?* Would you like to know where **Sandy Dennis** performed her teaching magic in *Up the Down Staircase* (1967)? If so, head to 899 10th Avenue,⑧ just two blocks north of 57th Street, to see a magnificent Flemish Renaissance–styled structure used in both films. Currently the John Jay College of Criminal Justice, the building until recently housed De Witt Clinton High School. Otherwise, our next stop is one block south and one east down 56th Street.

Director **Melvin Van Peebles** lives in the 353 West 56th Street⑨ building of the classic Parc Vendome. This pioneer of African-American cinema is finally receiving his well-deserved recognition.

At 333 West 56th Street,⑩ also a Parc Vendome address, resides acclaimed stage and film actress **Irene Worth.** Her neighbor in the building is another active stage actress, **Dee Hoty.** Tony Award–winning actress **Carole Shelley,** a Broadway fixture since her 1965 appearance in *The Odd Couple,* also has her home in this elegant complex brimming with major stars.

Need time to rest those weary legs? Relax on a wooden bench in a cute vest-pocket park at 8th Avenue and 56th Street. If you must quench that thirst immediately, walk ten feet to the Symphony Cafe, 950 Eighth Avenue (212-397-9595) which seconds as a clubhouse for Broadway stars such as **Dee Hoty** and **Keith Carra-dine.**  If it's late in the day, dress appropriately.

For those in need of nourishment, I have selected both a classic Italian restaurant and a less pricey yet attractive diner.

The Italian eatery happens to be **Frank Sinatra's** favorite. Frank and other celebrities enjoy the old-world service they receive from owners **Joe** and **Rose Scognamillo** at Patsy's, 236 West 56th Street (212-247-3491). These thoughtful restaurateurs even go so far as to receive mail for **Rush Limbaugh,** the controversial talk-show host.

• • •

talian cuisine expert **Al Pacino** *may have started a trend when he pulled up to Patsy's in a chauffeur-driven Jeep. Al enjoys dining in the establishment's secluded upper level.*

Around the corner and one block south, you find the Broadway Diner, an inexpensive restaurant that serves up some very tasty food. This neon-lighted Deco-style structure, which sits at 1726 Broadway (212-765-0909), counts a host of models, casting agents, and production people as its regular customers.

The diner is directly across Broadway from the home of blond-haired, blue-eyed **Jane Powell,** who lives at 230 West 55th Street.[10] An engaging personality, as well as nimble feet and a pleasing coloratura soprano voice, helped this fine actress-singer-dancer achieve movie stardom at an early age. She was born **Suzanne Burce,** but after appearing in the 1944 film *Song of the Open Road,* she decided to keep her character's name, Jane Powell.

RoseLand

When **Shirley MacLaine, Robert Duvall,** and **George Abbott** are in a cha-cha mood, they head straight to Roseland, 239 West 52nd Street, which is only three short blocks down Broadway and a few doors west on 52nd. **Fred Astaire** and **Ginger Rogers** referred to this legendary ballroom as "dance city." Look for the photos of **Elizabeth Taylor, Ann Miller,** and **Jane Powell** showcased under glass beneath this 1919 landmark's Las Vegas–style marquee.

Across the street at 240 West 52nd Street is a hangout for rock and rollers called the Lone Star Roadhouse. Major stars can often be found in the audience, listening to famous friends perform. **Bob Dylan** showed up recently to see buddy **Al Cooper** test new material. **Cyndi Lauper** got up from dinner to belt out a few tunes and **Kathleen Turner** sang a set or two with husband **Jay Weiss's** band, The Suits.

··· **B**··
*ad Boy" **Johnny Depp** punched his fist through a window and shattered glass in the face of a female patron at the Lone Star Roadhouse. The incident took place after a full day spent shooting a romantic comedy called* The Arrowtooth Waltz *on location in the bar. The young star, who also heard complaints about his nipping at the Jack Daniel's during filming, explained it as an accident.*
···

What do **Glenn Close, Richard Dreyfuss, Gene Hackman, Rob Lowe, Jessica Lange, Al Pacino, Alec Baldwin, Alan Alda, Joan Collins,** and **Debbie Gibson** have in common? Broadway. These singers and film stars are just a few of the many established performers who descend on the Great White Way to experience the excitement only the live stage can provide. With the hefty cost of theater production in the 1990s, "straight" plays (without music) don't get the press needed to survive unless their casts feature well-known names.

Times Square

Where better to start our Broadway tour than in front of the Neil Simon Theater, recently re-named to honor the most commercially successful playwright in American theater history. Known as the Alvin when it was built in 1927, this 250 West 52nd Street[12] structure opened with the Gershwins' smash hit *Funny Face,* starring **Fred Astaire.**

As you head deeper into the Broadway district, I'm positive you will be amazed by the abundance of quality productions offered in the area's almost forty theaters. Head back east to Broadway and make a left turn, heading northward one block.

To cite just a few, the Ed Sullivan Theater, 1697 Broadway,[13] was home to a number of famous CBS television variety shows, including those hosted by Jackie Gleason and Ed Sullivan. It was also the location of filming "Kate and Allie," the hit TV sitcom starring **Susan Saint James** and **Jane Curtin.** The theater is presently the showcase for CBS's David Letterman Show. Continue south on Broadway.

At 1681 Broadway,[14] the Broadway Theater has always managed to attract the most popular of musicals. **Barbra Streisand** appeared there in *Funny Girl.* **Yul Brynner** starred in the revival of *The King and I,* and in 1987 *Les Misérables* opened to rave reviews and a long run. Two blocks down, at 1634 Broadway,[15] is the Winter Garden, which opened with **Al Jolson** in 1911 and more recently featured the seemingly endless run of *Cats.* Sixteen thirty-three Broadway[16] is where you'll find the Gershwin Theater. This spacious auditorium was built in 1972, but its short span has been graced by an abundance of major stars, including **Frank Sinatra, Sammy Davis, Jr., Rudolf Nureyev,** and **Linda Ronstadt.**

Why pay full price for a Broadway show? At TKTS (47th Street and Broadway), you can purchase a ticket at half of its face-value cost (plus a small service charge) for same-day performances. Don't be surprised if you stand next to a cost-conscious celebrity while waiting on line to make

T.K.T.S., 47th & Broadway

your selection. Make a right on 46th Street to reach our next destination.

The Paramount Hotel, 235 West 46th Street, is the newly renovated theater-district habitat favored by young trendy stars when they visit the Big Apple. One evening, **Harry Connick, Jr.** opted to stay here after a performance at the nearby Lunt-Fontanne Theater (205 West 46th Street) rather than return to his Greenwich Village home. **Cher** took over the basement, which had been **Billy Rose's** Diamond Horseshoe Club during Prohibition, to launch her new perfume. It was rumored **Madonna** tried to purchase that same basement not long after. If you need to use a pay phone, head past the Armani-suited doormen into the chicly furnished lobby, where you'll use Mr. Bell's invention while you savor the smell of fresh roses. Flowers are placed daily in the toilet-roll holders located in the bathrooms only a few feet away.

When movie stars go club hopping, they're no longer content to sit at the best table in the house; now, they want to own it. **Matt Dillon** is one of the latest to follow this trend. The young star's stylish watering hole—called The Whiskey—in the Paramount Hotel is a favorite night spot for the likes of **Sean Young, Robert De Niro, Madonna, Spike Lee,** and **Julia Roberts.**

T H E W H I S K E Y

··· **A** ···
*drunk attempting to steal a circus stool, used as a foot-stool at the chic Whiskey Bar, was shocked when superhero **Robocop** sprang into action and apprehended the culprit. The silver screen came to life when **Peter Weller** decided to portray his hit film character after spotting corruption in Gotham.*

···

Walk to 8th Avenue, make a left, then make another left on 44th Street to reach our next stop. While Sardi's, 234 West 44th Street, [17] (212-221-8440) is not the meeting place it once was for theatrical stars, agents, and producers, you can get a feel for the restaurant's former glory by seeing the caricatures of Broadway actors that cover its walls. **Ellen Barkin** has a romantic rendezvous with a beautiful cosmetic-company president in Sardi's while playing a male turned female in the film *Switch* (1991).

Sardi's, 234 W. 44th Street

Head south to 43rd and one long block west to the corner of 9th Avenue. On the southwest corner is the home of veteran actor **Jack Warden** in a luxury high rise just off the Broadway strip at 400 West 43rd Street. [18] Walk west to the far corner of the same block and you arrive at a similar-looking complex, which is home to popular television, film, and stage actress **Angela Lansbury.** Her residence at 484 West 43rd Street [19] is also home to rising film actor **Eric Douglas,** youngest son of Hollywood legend **Kirk Douglas.**

Angela Lansbury

SARDI'S

Around the corner and several doors west, at 529 West 42nd Street,[20] in a renovated warehouse-type complex, lives singer-actress **Maureen McGovern.** Her Academy Award–winning pop sound helped her achieve a lifelong dream when in 1989 she debuted at Carnegie Hall.

Gotham's Madison Square Garden has recently emerged as prime stargazing territory. **Bill Cosby, Anthony Quinn, Woody Allen, Kathleen Turner,** and **Rob Lowe** trek to this sports palace to cheer on coach **Pat Riley** and his New York Knickerbocker basketball team. **John McEnroe, Ahmad Rashad,** and **Spike Lee** each forked out $12,900 for a season's worth of courtside seats. Celebrities are also on hand at Ranger hockey games and other major sporting events, as well as the Barnum & Bailey Circus every spring. The precast concrete Garden complex is located between West 31st and West 33rd streets, from 7th to 8th avenues. Twenty minutes walking, five to ten minutes by bus, or a $3.50 cab ride will place you there. If you decide to walk, head east on 42nd Street to 8th Avenue, make a right, and nine short blocks later you will be at your destination.

Otherwise, our next stop is Chelsea, the neighborhood where America's movie industry began in 1912 at Zukor's Famous Players Studio, with stars including **John Barrymore and Mary Pickford.** This richly ethnic middle-class area is home to New York Actors Studio–trained **Rip Torn.** Rip's residence at 435 West 22nd Street[21] might take close to half an hour on foot, but a bus or taxi would get you there in minutes. Straight down 10th Avenue and a left turn on 22nd Street is the most direct route from 42nd Street. Take 8th Avenue south to 22nd Street, then walk one and a half blocks west if you're coming from Madison Square Garden.

Up until his death in September of 1992, **Anthony Perkins** resided around the corner, at 467 West 21st Street.[22] The actor's town house is deceptively plain-looking, considering the neurotic and sometimes terrifying character portrayals that were his specialty in films such as Alfred Hitchcock's *Psycho* (1960).

It's no accident **Anthony Perkins** was so convincing as so many mentally unstable characters. His father's premature death and mother's excessive demands brought him at age thirty-four to Manhattan psychotherapist **Mildred Newman.** The doctor helped Anthony conquer his fears.

Anthony Perkins

Another block south and around the corner, in a small brick building at 434 West 20th Street,[23] resides actress **Blair Brown,** star of the television sitcom "The Days and Nights of Molly Dodd." The offbeat series, now playing in rerun on cable, has become a cult favorite.

The Chelsea Hotel

Head three blocks north on 9th Avenue and one and a half east to reach the Chelsea Hotel, 222 West 23rd Street.[24] Over the years, its residential roster has read like a Who's Who in American Letters. A sampling includes **Mark Twain, Dylan Thomas, Bob Dylan, Sid Vicious, Arthur Miller,** and **Eugene O'Neill.** The hotel's Bohemian atmosphere inspired resident **William Burroughs** to write *Naked Lunch* and **Arthur Clarke** to give birth to his screenplay for *2001: A Space Odyssey* (1968), based on his book of the same name. This 1884 pink brick building with its intricately woven iron grillwork was designated in 1966 as New York landmark.

Twenty-third Street between 7th and 8th avenues is a perfect location to end the tour, since both subway and bus routes are close at hand. If you walk to 8th Avenue, you can take the A, C, or E train; on 7th Avenue, you'll find the 1, 2, 3, or 9. Crosstown buses are available on 23rd Street.

TOUR 4

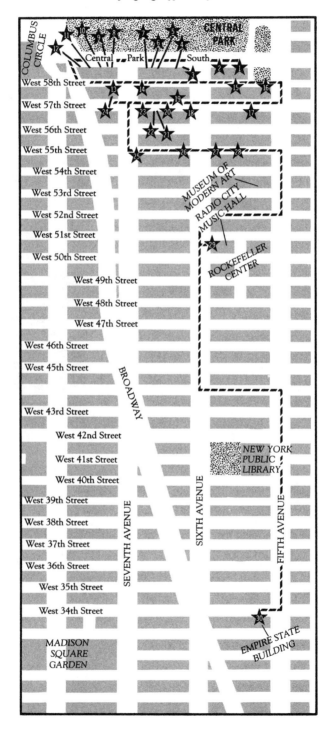

CELEBRITY NOSH
CENTRAL PARK SOUTH

STARS IN THE AREA

Warren Beatty ☆ Candice Bergen ☆ Christie Brinkley ☆ Larry Hagman ☆ La Toya Jackson ☆ Billy Joel ☆ Luciano Pavarotti ☆ Lynn Redgrave ☆ Telly Savalas ☆ Raquel Welch

NUMBER	ADDRESS	NAME
1	5th Avenue and 59th Street	*Home Alone 2*
		The Way We Were
		Plaza Suite
		Arthur
		Crocodile Dundee
		North by Northwest
		The Great Gatsby
		Network
		The Cotton Club
		The Pickle
2	36 Central Park South	Leona Helmsley
		Harry Helmsley
3	106 Central Park South	La Toya Jackson
		O. J. Simpson
		Larry Hagman
		Morton Downey, Jr.
4	112 Central Park South	Warren Beatty
		Annette Bening
5	128 Central Park South	Billy Joel
		Christie Brinkley
6	150 Central Park South	Luciano Pavarotti
		Placido Domingo
		Milos Forman
		Ingrid Bergman (deceased)
		Frank Sinatra
		Ava Gardner (deceased)
7	160 Central Park South	Telly Savalas
		George Burns
		Bing Crosby (deceased)
		Betty Grable (deceased)
		Lily Pons (deceased)
		Rudy Vallee (deceased)

8	200 Central Park South	**Raquel Welch** **Melba Moore** **Dino De Laurentiis** **Doris Roberts**
9	210 Central Park South	**Mary Higgins Clark** **Keith Hernandez**
10	220 Central Park South	**Don Hewitt**
11	222 Central Park South	**Candice Bergen** **Louis Malle**
12	240 Central Park South	**Bill Boggs** **Sylvia Miles** **Lou Jacobi**
13	200 West 58th Street	**Michael Moriarty** **Buster Poindexter**
14	180 West 58th Street	**Rita Gam** **Natasha Richardson**
15	42 West 58th Street	**Hume Cronyn** **Jessica Tandy** **Carol Burnett**
16	754 5th Avenue	*Arthur* *Just Tell Me What You* *Want*
17	60 West 57th Street	**Jerzy Kosinski** (deceased)
18	100 West 57th Street	**Alexandra Danilova** **John Gabriel**
19	111 West 57th Street	**Joan Sutherland**
20	130 West 57th Street	**John Oates**
21	146 West 57th Street	**Martin Scorsese**
22	150 West 57th Street	*Tootsie* *Manhattan* *The Turning Point*

23	152–160 West 57th Street	**Marlon Brando** **Leonard Bernstein** (deceased) **John Barrymore** (deceased) **Isadora Duncan** (deceased)
24	205 West 57th Street	**Lynn Redgrave** **Jeffrey Lyons** **Fran Liebowitz** **André Watts** **Gig Young** (deceased)
25	853 7th Avenue	**John Heard** **Mary Travers**
26	101 West 55th Street	**Tony Bennett**

27	77 West 55th Street	**Henny Youngman**
28	24 West 55th Street	**Hal David**
29	1260 Avenue of the Americas	*Annie Hall*
		Radio Days
		The Godfather
30	350 5th Avenue	*Love Affair*
		King Kong
		On the Town
		An Affair to Remember

The perfect time for stargazers to spot their favorite celebrities is during lunch or dinner at one of Manhattan's glamorous or trendy restaurants. This area contains an amazing mix of hot new eateries as well as older, more established gourmet dining spots.

Our tour begins at the Plaza Hotel, perennial host to a vast array of stars and a favorite setting for filmmakers, and culminates at the Empire State Building, scene of the city's most memorable depiction on film. The residence buildings occupied by celebrities tend to cluster within a five-block square south of Central Park. This vast landscaped park offers a moment of tranquility to New Yorkers eager to escape the agitation and turmoil of their glamorous but frenetic concrete jungle.

The area covered on this tour is bounded by Broadway on the west, 5th Avenue on the east, Central Park South on the north, and 34th Street on the south.

Starting Address:	**5th Avenue at 59th Street**
Length of Tour:	**1 Hour, 45 Minutes**
Best Starting Time:	**10:00 A.M., 12:00 P.M., or 5:00 P.M.**
Subway:	**N or R to 5th Avenue**
Bus:	**1, 5, or 30**
Bring Along:	**Opera glasses, Donald Trump's book *The Art of the Deal*, and, if you plan on stepping into the Carnegie Deli, Tums for the tummy**

☆ THE TOUR

Fifth Avenue and 60th Street (N or R train) is a short block south from the start of our tour. Point your feet in the direction of the flags on the second-floor balcony of the Plaza Hotel that represent countries of important foreign guests and within minutes you'll arrive at this world-famous complex.

The Plaza Hotel, 5th Avenue and 59th Street,⓵ has hosted more stars, and been featured in more of their movies, than any other building in Gotham. The hotel's popularity with the rich and famous is understandable considering its spectacular view of Central Park, its majestic exterior and elegant interior, and the constant traffic of horse-drawn carriages catering to incurable romantics.

While putting final touches on this tour, I was astonished to pass a gigantic pickle at the entrance to the Plaza. No ordinary side dish, the monstrous half-sour was playing the title role in *The Pickle,* a film starring **Danny Aiello** and directed by **Paul Mazursky.** At the same time, the Plaza's parkside face was providing the cinematic escape route for New York's own **Macaulay Culkin** as he fled bumbling burglars **Joe Pesci** and **Daniel Stern** in *Home Alone 2*, sequel to the young star's original box-office smash.

··· **P**··
erhaps **Macaulay Culkin** *and superstar agent* **Sam Cohn** *can persuade the youth's parents that at $15 million per film the child superstar earns enough to have his own bedroom. Macaulay resides in a four-room apartment on the Upper East Side with mom, Pat, dad, Kit, and six (count 'em, six) siblings.*

··

The Plaza Hotel

The many memorable films in which the Plaza Hotel appears include *North by Northwest* (1959), *The Way We Were* (1973), *The Great Gatsby* (1974), *Network* (1976) *Arthur* (1981), *The Cotton Club* (1984), "*Crocodile*" *Dundee* (1986), and, of course, *Plaza Suite* (1971).

The Plaza, a creation of architect Henry Janeway Hardenbergh, who also designed the star-studded Dakota, is owned by **Donald Trump,** who has instituted a massive restoration of the structure. "The Donald," as he's known to readers of New York gossip columns, promises to make this landmark "the greatest hotel in the world."

Continue walking west, down the block from the Plaza, to the Park Lane Hotel, 36 Central Park South, ② home to New York's Hotel Queen, **Leona Helmsley.** Leona and her husband, **Harry,** own this forty-six-story limestone hotel, as well as dozens of other prestigious New York hotels and office buildings.

... **A**..
*dded to billionairess **Leona Helmsley's** lavish homes in New York, Florida, and Arizona is her government-sponsored residence in a crowded prison dormitory at the Federal Medical Center in Lexington, Kentucky. The Queen may have regretted her comment that "Only little people pay taxes" after Judge Thomas Griesa sentenced her in 1992 to four years' imprisonment for income-tax evasion, a crime of which she was convicted in a 1988 trial.*
....

Baseball legend **Mickey Mantle** is often on hand signing autographs for patrons at his 42 Central Park South bistro. Mickey Mantle's Restaurant and Sports Bar (212-688-7777) is a popular hangout for present-day athletes, sports stars of yesteryear, and well-dressed fans hoping to mingle with their playing-field heroes. If you happen by on a Tuesday or Thursday between 12:00 and 2:00 P.M., stop in and enjoy a taping for all-sports radio station WFAN. Walk farther west to the St. Moritz Hotel, 50 Central Park South, and stop in for a treat at Rumpelmayer's. It's a world-renowned soda shop. Cross over Avenue of the Americas.

Rumpelmayer's, 50 Central Park South

Luxurious Trump Parc, 106 Central Park South, ③ with its vast terraces and elegant lobby, is one of the town's hottest new buildings for major celebrities. The complex was created from the steel shell of the former Barbizon Hotel by—who else?—developer **Donald Trump.**

Snake charmer and singing sensation **La Toya Jackson** lives the good life in her beautiful Trump Parc residence. Her neighbor in the building is actor, sports commentator, and Hall of Fame halfback **O. J. Simpson.** Perhaps O.J. leaps down the Trump Parc's lengthy halls when he practices for his airport car-rental commercials.

One hundred six Central Park South is also home to actor **Larry Hagman,** J.R. in the 1980s nighttime soap classic "Dallas." Larry was chosen to be the man America loved to hate after starring on the daytime "Edge of Night." If you see a pair of bright red socks walking around Trump Parc, they just might be on the feet of former controversial talk-show host **Morton Downey, Jr.**

Warren Beatty

The Ritz-Carlton, next door at 112 Central Park South, ④ which was renovated and reopened in 1982, is the home of movie heartthrob **Warren Beatty** and his new family. Prior to Warren's career as leading man in films like *Bonnie and Clyde* (1967) and *Shampoo* (1975), he pocketed extra cash as a bricklayer's helper on the Lincoln Tunnel construction crew while studying acting with New York's **Stella Adler.** Warren interrupted his long-running bachelor party in March of 1992 to marry gorgeous actress **Annette Bening,** the mother of his first child. The couple lighted up the screen with their erotic exploits in the 1991 hit film *Bugsy,* and they will most definitely excite onlookers when they stroll from this fashionable home on Central Park South.

Christie Brinkley   *Billy Joel*

Continue west on Central Park South a few doors. Rock legend **Billy Joel** calls the classic building at 128 Central Park South⑤ home. Billy occupies the penthouse unit with his wife, supermodel **Christie Brinkley.** If there is ever any problem with the hot water, the only person Billy can complain to is himself, since this savvy investor owns the entire building. Residents tell of how warm and unassuming their rock-and-roll landlord is, while the gorgeous Christie is always guarded and aloof.

· · · **B**··
illy Joel directed the elevator operator at 128 Central Park South to stop at the penthouse. Unaware of his passenger's identity, the worker stared into the singer's eyes and asked, "Don't you know that Billy Joel lives there?" Billy smiled and answered yes in order not to embarrass the man.
· ·

Our next stop heading west is the elegant Hampshire House at 150 Central Park South,⑥ home to **Luciano Pavarotti,** the man *Newsweek* magazine dubbed "opera's greatest turn-on." After weighing in at a rotund three hundred pounds, this five eleven tenor has resolved to crash-diet. The hungry singer will try to curb his appetite by forsaking

Luciano Pavarotti

his favorite eatery, the San Domenico, 240 Central Park South. Luciano's colleague—and rival for the title of world's greatest tenor—**Placido Domingo** lives in the building, as well.

The musical theme of the Hampshire House is further apparent with the presence of another world-class artist, Academy Award–winning movie director **Milos Forman.** Especially adept at bringing Broadway hits to the silver screen, his version of the sixties musical *Hair* (1979) was largely filmed in the oasis across the street—Central Park.

Ingrid Bergman, Frank Sinatra, and **Ava Gardner** had homes in the Hampshire House back in the 1940s and 1950s.

···**F**··

rank Sinatra's *infamous romantic rendezvous with* **Ava Gardner** *is a Hampshire House legend. In 1950, "Old Blue Eyes" took a suite on the eighth floor and Ava took one down the hall. (In town to sing at the Copa, then New York's top night spot, Frank had left his wife, Nancy, back in California.) The stars' privacy was soon lost, however, as word of their love nest leaked out and the Hampshire House was invaded by nosy journalists looking to sniff out the story.*

··

The Essex House, next door at 160 Central Park South, ⑦ has recently undergone a $75 million renovation to restore its original Art Deco splendor. Celebrities are once again looking to purchase homes in this prestigious hotel-condo complex. **David Bowie,** I'm told, may soon be the owner of an Essex House residence suite.

Presently, the best-known resident of the Essex House is TV detective and native New Yorker **Telly Savalas.** As you pass the building, see whether you can detect a bald, stocky man sucking on a lollipop.

Among the many alluring residents of the Essex House in the past have been **Bing Crosby, Rudy Vallee, Betty Grable,** and **George Burns.** But for sheer animal magnetism, none surpassed the jaguar owned by **Lily Pons:** The pa-

The Essex House
160 Central Park South

trician pet pussy cat was given free reign to roam throughout the legendary soprano's luxury suite.

True to its name, Les Célébrités, (212-484-5113) the intimate French restaurant located on the first floor of the Essex House, features artwork by celebrities. Artists whose paintings are displayed on its walls include **Gene Hackman, Sally Struthers, James Dean, Phyllis Diller,** and **Sally Kirkland.** If your home isn't complete without a painting of **David Bowie** by **Claire Trevor,** it's available for purchase—at a gourmet price.

Raquel Welch resides at 200 Central Park South, [8] at the southwest corner of 7th Avenue, in an unusually shapely edifice. Art imitates life, and vice versa, as the extravagant curves of the building's facade remind one of the swooping lines that are the trademark of this ageless sex goddess.

Raquel's neighbor at 200 Central Park South is singer-actress **Melba Moore,** who is Big Apple–born and raised. Another building resident is **Dino De Laurentiis,** the larger-than-

Raquel Welch

life movie mogul. A familiar face you might also spot here is that of television actress **Doris Roberts,** whose work has earned her a pair of Emmys.

Next door, at 210 Central Park South [9] resides one of America's best-selling suspense writers, **Mary Higgins Clark.** If this superb storyteller needs ideas for a mystery novel involving diamonds—of the baseball variety, that is—she should contact first baseman **Keith Hernandez,** who also lives here. Continue west on Central Park South.

New York–born **Don Hewitt,** producer of "60 Minutes" for CBS, has his home at 220 Central Park South. [10]

The Gainsborough Studios at 222 Central Park South [11] is a building that was opened in 1907 to house up-and-coming artists. The structure's unique facade is mosaic and is topped by a bust of Thomas Gainsborough. No doubt the eighteenth-century English portraitist would have enjoyed rendering on canvas the classic beauty of **Candice Bergen,** otherwise known as Murphy Brown. She and her husband, film director **Louis Malle,** live here with their daughter, **Chloe.** Candace had all but given up on men when she found her Prince Charming.

··· **C**andice Bergen *played the role of* **Sydney Biddle Barrows** *in the 1987 television movie* Mayflower Madam. *Sydney, whose ancestors were indeed among the Pilgrims who landed at Plymouth Rock, ran New York's classiest call-girl operation from her home at 304 West 74th Street (until 1984, when the law finally paid a call on her). So the home of this real-life madam is just blocks from that of the actress who played her in film. Only in Manhattan.*

When stars such as **Roberta Flack, Cyndi Lauper, Mary Travers,** and **Norman Lear** visit the dentist, they expect amenities like a television in every room. They get them at 230 Central Park South from **Marc G. Lowenberg, D.D.S., P.C.** Cosmetic dentist to the stars, Dr. Marc has a patient roster that includes many celebrities. The in-office entertainment can present unusual risks, however, especially when tuned to MTV: Marc remembers the time Roberta Flack began "bopping" to her own video while in the chair.

Newsman **Bill Boggs** might have chosen 240 Central Park South[12] as his home after discovering that fellow journalist Lois Lane lived there in the movie *Superman.* More likely, he was drawn to the structure's super, and oh-so-sophisticated, architecture.

New York native **Sylvia Miles,** who studied acting at the Actors Studio, also calls 240 Central Park South home, as does veteran stage and film actor **Lou Jacobi.**

At the same address, you'll also find the San Domenico restaurant (212-265-5959). This colorful yet elegant Italian eatery is frequented by stars like **Michael Douglas, Harry Belafonte, Candice Bergen,** and **Christopher Plummer.** Lucky Christopher: While dining at the restaurant a few weeks back, he happened to bump into producer **Douglas Cramer,** who signed him on the spot to star in an upcoming flick.

Walk a few yards west to the edge of Columbus Circle. Within view is an odd-shaped white marble building housing the New York City Department of Cultural Affairs. The ground floor contains an information center that offers free handouts on cultural events, sites, and attractions. Continue around the corner, south to 58th Street, turn left, and head one block east to the corner of 7th Avenue.

At 200 West 58th Street,[13] resides Tony and Emmy Award–winning actor **Michael Moriarty.** A gifted jazz pianist

Award–winning actor **Michael Moriarty.** A gifted jazz pianist as well, Michael gigged around town early in his career at a variety of night spots. In the same complex resides fellow actor and fellow music maker **Buster Poindexter.**

Across the street, the Alwyn Court, 180 West 58th Street,⑭ built in 1909 with the beautiful splendor of the French Renaissance, is one of the most appealing buildings in Manhattan. The exterior detailing is terra-cotta woven like a tapestry.

Actress **Rita Gam** grew up in Manhattan and presently resides in the Alwyn Court. Her neighbor there is movie star **Natasha Richardson,** owner of one of acting's most dazzling pedigrees: Her father was English stage director **Tony Richardson,** and her mother, **Vanessa,** and maternal aunt, **Lynn,** are both performers surnamed **Redgrave,** as was her grandfather **Michael.**

··· **W**hen *Rita Gam decided that writing was more challenging than acting, she began submitting ideas to publishing houses, only to be rejected time and again. Finally, after confining herself to a rigorous writing schedule in her beautiful and spacious apartment, she wrote the book* Actress to Actress. *Rita achieves success a bit more easily now, as both actress and writer.*

Heading east on 58th Street, back toward 5th Avenue, we pass the popular Wyndham Hotel, 42 West 58th Street,⑮ home to husband-and-wife acting greats **Hume Cronyn** and **Jessica Tandy.** While Jessica's performance in the movie *Driving Miss Daisy* (1989) earned her an Oscar at the age of eighty, she and Hume are most beloved for their work on the Broadway stage. For the half century each has spent on the Great White Way, both

Hume Cronyn

have been honored with induction into the Theater Hall of Fame.

Actress-comedienne **Carol Burnett,** who for years was glad to have time together with millions of American TV viewers, also keeps a residence at the Wyndham. A half-block stroll eastward along 58th Street to the corner of 5th Avenue takes us to our next stop.

Stargazing at the store the rich and famous call their own requires little skill. Entertainers **Candice Bergen** and **Cher** and socialites **Ann Bass** and **Ivana Trump** are just a few of the celebrities who stroll the aisles at Bergdorf Goodman, 754 5th Avenue.[16] But shopping can be so exhausting! When Ivana needs to resupply her costmetics shelf, she let's her fingers do the walking. She phones Bergdorf's Mary Kavanagh, who personally delivers the goods to Ivana's Trump Tower luxury suite.

Liza Minelli shoplifted a tie for her father from Bergdorf Goodman in the 1981 film *Arthur.* The store was no less prominent in *Just Tell Me What You Want,* the 1980 film starring **Ali MacGraw.**

Around the corner and west a few buildings, at 37 West 57th Street, is Harry Stewart's, where film actors are wardrobed for leading roles. Harry himself designed the outfits worn by **Robert De Niro** and **Joe Pesci** in *Goodfellas* and **Harrison Ford** in *Regarding Henry.* According to this star suit maker, the tailored look of the thirties will make a return engagement in the nineties.

Continue west on 57th Street to 60 West 57th Street,[17] the building author **Jerzy Kosinski** lived in until his death in 1991. While being there, he authored the Oscar-winning screenplay *Being There,* based on his novel of the same name.

A bit farther west, at 100 West 57th Street (corner of the Avenue of the Americas),[18] resides prima ballerina and

Ritz Thrift Shop, 107 W. 57th Street

choreographer **Alexandra Danilova.** Currently on the faculty of the School of American Ballet, Alexandra gives lecture tours around the world. Also at home here is talented actor **John Gabriel.** Continue west.

You don't have to be a movie star to dress like one. Today, it's chic for stars and jet-setters to buy and sell their fur coats at the Ritz Thrift Shop, 107 West 57th Street. Stop in for a glass of champagne and bargain for that touch of mink. Buyers and sellers here have included **Joanne Woodward, Virginia Graham, Mrs. Johnny Cash,** and **Sally Jessy Raphael.** Your cut-rate purchase might net you a profit sooner than you realize: One shopper recently found money stuffed in her new coat's shoulder pad.

··· **W**·······························
hat would you do if the name **Jackie Kennedy** *was sewn on the inside of the autumn-haze mink you just bought? The customer who purchased the former First Lady's fur didn't hesitate: "Take it out," she ordered the saleswoman. "I wear my own labels."*
·····························

Soprano **Joan Sutherland** found her way to Carnegie Hall by practice, practice, practice. But to get there on short notice the diva needed living quarters close by, so she moved into 111 West 57th Street.[19] Joan's coloratura, which has thrilled opera fans around the world, is especially appreciated in this most musical of cities, where she has made countless appearances at both Carnegie Hall and Lincoln Center. Keep your feet moving west.

When **John Oates** composed his hot-selling pop tune "Rich Girl," he must have been eyeing the chick crowd ambling past 130 West 57th Street,[20] where he has his opulent abode. John moved to New York in 1971 with partner **Daryl Hall** in search of a recording contract, and since then the rock duo **Hall and Oates** has had one hit after another.

What do **Bruce Willis, Arnold Schwarzenegger,** and **Sly Stallone** have in common? A snazzy new hamburger joint called Planet Hollywood at 140 West 57th Street (212-333-7827). Celebrities attending the opening of this mecca of movie memorabilia included **Kim Basinger** and companion, **Alec Baldwin, Michael J. Fox, Stevie Wonder, Glenn**

Close, and **Don Johnson.** The restaurant has a private screening room, a favorite place for stars to munch popcorn as they preview their most recent film. Continue west toward 7th Avenue.

Director **Martin Scorsese** believes that the reality of his life, which includes being raised in a tenement in New York's Little Italy, entering and dropping out of seminary, studying and teaching film at New York University, and now living in an elegant residence at 146 West 57th Street,[21] is interchangeable with the reality of his films. If you consider his fleeing the mean streets of Little Italy by hailing a taxi driver and directing him to the center of New York, New York, this raging bull who created *The Last Temptation of Christ* certainly has a life that parallels his art.

If you hunger to see celebrities sipping borscht while they make deals (stopping only to air-kiss new arrivals—always on both cheeks), then the Russian Tea Room (212-265-0947) at 150 West 57th Street[22] is a definite stop. Limousines begin pulling up around 1:00 P.M., dropping off superstars to make any stargazer salivate. **Michael Douglas, Dustin Hoffman, Alan King, Woody Allen, Carol Channing, Paul Newman,** and **Candice Bergen** are a few of the celebrity elite for whom the middle eight booths are reserved. By the way, don't be confused if you see tinsel and holly in July—the colorful Christmas decorations stay up year-round at this brownstone eatery, which was built in 1870.

The Russian Tea Room has been used as a backdrop in many films. **Dustin Hoffman,** in drag, shocked director **Sydney Pollack** by revealing his true identity while the two were lunching in a middle booth in *Tootsie* (1982). **Woody Allen,** a big fan of the blinis, brought his son to the Tea Room in *Manhattan* (1979). The restaurant was also featured in *The Turning Point* (1977), starring **Shirley MacLaine** and **Anne Bancroft,** two of the establishment's most devoted regulars.

• • • **L**ook, *this is **Paul Newman.** You'd better come see my daughter," said this proud father when he manned the phone lines at the Russian Tea Room. Paul's daughter Melissa was booked for a performance in the restaurant on cabaret night.*

Carnegie Hall has been the stage for entertainment's elite since it was built in 1891 by philanthropist **Andrew Carnegie.** For some stars, however, the structure has provided a home, as well. Above this Italian Renaissance–designed building at 152–160 West 57th Street[23] are residences that have housed **Marlon Brando, Leonard Bernstein, John Barrymore,** and **Isadora Duncan.** Television specials are frequently set in Carnegie Hall's white auditorium to take advantage of its world-renowned acoustics. Two versions of the feature film *Unfaithfully Yours* (1948 and 1984), about a symphony orchestra conductor who suspects his wife of infidelity, also centered on the concert hall. Our next stop is across the road on the northwest corner of 57th Street and 7th Avenue.

The Osborne, 205 West 57th Street,[24] has long been a popular residence for painters, musicians, actors, and other people involved in the arts. The building's solid, sound-resistant construction, proximity to Carnegie Hall, fifteen-foot ceilings, and ornately decorated lobby all add to its appeal.

Residing in the Renaissance palazzo–styled building is the very successful stage and screen actress **Lynn Redgrave.** Another resident, in his very own "Lyon's den," is film critic **Jeffrey Lyons,** son of **Leonard Lyons,** for decades a top New York entertainment columnist. His neighbor in the building is sardonic author **Fran Lebowitz,** considered by the *Washington Post* to be "the funniest woman in America." Rounding out the Osborne's current celebrity registry is **André Watts,** the famed American pianist.

The solidly constructed Osborne came apart in 1978 when the bodies of Oscar–winning actor **Gig Young** and his beautiful wife, **Kim Schmidt,** were discovered in his home in the building. Perhaps the frustrations of his long Hollywood career had finally caught up with him when he shot himself and his wife of three weeks.

Now might be a perfect moment to freshen up, rest your weary legs, and fill your empty tummy. How about a hot, lean skyscraper of a corned beef sandwich at the best deli in town? The Carnegie Deli, 854 7th Avenue, (212-757-2245) is

a hangout for comic greats that include **Goldie Hawn, Woody Allen, Bill Cosby,** and **Milton Berle. Henny Youngman** has lunch there every day. An unusual feature of the deli, not common among Big Apple restaurants, is its insistence that stars stand in line like anyone else. The restaurant honors its most famous customers by naming sandwiches after them. (Example: "The Woody Allen, for the dedicated fresser only! Lotsa corned beef plus lotsa pastrami.") From 57th Street, the restaurant is a couple of blocks south, down 7th Avenue, just below 55th Street.

Close by at 853 7th Avenue[25] is the home of actor **John Heard.** The building also houses **Mary Travers,** still active in the singing group **Peter, Paul and Mary.**

We now journey east on 55th Street one block to 101 West 55th Street,[26] where New York–born singer **Tony Bennett** resides. Tony studied at New York's High School of Industrial Art to be a commercial artist but switched to a singing career when he was discovered performing in local pasta joints. Continue east.

"King of the One-liners" **Henny Youngman,** whose trademarks are his violin and his line "Take my wife—Please," lives at 77 West 55th Street.[27] Only a few doors farther east, at 24 West 55th Street,[28] is world-renowned lyricist **Hal David.** We now head to 5th Avenue, turn right, and right again on 54th Street.

Scandal ensued at 13 West 54th Street after former **Governor** and **Vice President Nelson Rockefeller** died of a heart attack in his town house while "working" with his assistant, **Megan Marshak.** The story got juicy when the press discovered that Megan waited an hour before reporting the death. Head back to 5th Avenue and stroll south to 52nd Street, where we'll turn right.

Just off 5th Avenue at 21 West 52nd Street is the "21" Club (212-582-7200), a restaurant frequented by the most famous and powerful people in the world. You might want to stop for a drink at the bar, which overlooks an elegant dining area frequented by the likes of **Lauren Bacall, Warren Beatty, Elizabeth Taylor,** and **Frank Sinatra,** plus a host of others. Years back, when Frank Sinatra and Lauren Bacall arrived for dinner on the same evening, the maître d' was instructed to seat them "as far apart as geographically possible." It seems Frank had dropped her cold after the two had been talking marriage only a few days before. This onetime speakeasy has been immortalized in film. In the 1950 film *All About Eve*, **Bette Davis** lunches at "21," while more recently **Michael Douglas** talks business here with **Charlie Sheen** in *Wall Street* (1987). Continue west on 52nd Street to the corner, which is the Avenue of the Americas, turn left, and head south two blocks to our next location.

Radio City Music Hall
1260 Avenue of the Americas

If you spot several stoic-looking men wearing earphones and blocking your view of a row of cast-iron jockey statues in front of the "21" Club, it must be President's Night. One recent evening, a very sleepy **Ronald Reagan** and his very glamorous wife, **Nancy,** sat at a table near the bar. The couple and the chef, also a former actor, discussed their most recent careers. I watched the conversation from the bar, glued to my seat by the icy stares of three Secret Service agents—I was held captive by my fear of being shot while grabbing for my wallet to pay the bill.

Twelve sixty Avenue of the Americas[29] is Radio City Music Hall, home to the **Rockettes.** This cavernous theater, with its extravagant Art Deco lobby, was built in the early years of the Depression and has staged some of the most spectacular performances in show-business history. Films featuring Radio City have included **Woody Allen's** *Annie Hall* (1977) and *Radio Days* (1987), plus **Francis Ford Coppola's** *The Godfather* (1972). If you have the time, Radio City offers an hour-long backstage tour. Check at the box office or call 212-632-4041.

NBC Studios, 30 Rockefeller Plaza

If you passed Radio City Music Hall in the early part of 1992 and saw a number of sheep being herded by two dogs into a waiting taxi, cancel that extra visit to your therapist. The stunt was performed for the taping of "David Letterman's Tenth Anniversary Special."

Across the street at 30 Rockefeller Plaza (southeast corner of 50th Street and the Avenue of the Americas) are the NBC Studios, where the television show "Saturday Night Live" is produced before a live studio audience. The scenic Rainbow Room restaurant, located on the sixty-fifth floor, is the romantic setting in the film *The Prince of Tides* (1991) for a steamy encounter between psychiatrist **Barbra Streisand** and her semipatient **Nick Nolte.** NBC invites you to take a tour of television studios for a small fee (212-664-7174).

The Royalton Hotel

... **A** *surprised* **Eddie Murphy** *stepped out of his limousine into a pile of horse manure. The comedian decided to slip out of his $500 loafers and walk shoeless up to his job at NBC Studios as star of "Saturday Night Live."*

Heading south down the Avenue of the Americas, we pass the Diamond District (West 47th Street, between 5th Avenue and the Avenue of the Americas), where more than $400 million worth of diamonds are traded daily. The danger and excitement of the street led director **Sidney Lumet** to use it in filming *Stranger Among Us* (1992), starring **Melanie Griffith** as an undercover cop. Continue walking to 44th Street, turn left, and head to the middle of the block.

The Hotel Algonquin, 59 West 44th Street, is the first of three hotels we shall visit that have catered to famous writers, actors, and lyricists. The Algonquin, with its elegantly paneled lobby, was the home of the celebrated Round Table, a group that in the 1920s convened daily for lunch at a round table in the main dining room. Writer **Dorothy Parker,** playwright **George S. Kaufman,** and actress **Tallulah Bankhead** were members of this formidable gathering of young, bright, and talented people. Film star **Douglas Fairbanks, Sr.,** had a residence in the hotel between 1908 and 1915, as did novelist **F. Scott Fitzgerald** throughout the 1930s. Two films featuring the Hotel Algonquin include director **Otto Preminger's** suspense thriller *Laura* (1944) and *Rich and Famous*, a 1981 drama starring **Jacqueline Bissett** and **Candice Bergen.**

James Dean entertained guests in the lobby of the Hotel Algonquin, but as a struggling young actor in the early 1950s he could afford to live only in the less expensive Iroquois Hotel, next door at 49 West 44th Street. James shared room 802 with friend and fellow actor **William Bast.**

Across the road, the Royalton Hotel, 44 West 44th Street, has undergone a multimillion-dollar refurbishment and is recapturing its former glory as a celebrity meeting place. The block-long futuristically designed lobby attracts stars including **Madonna, Sean Penn, Billy Baldwin,** and **Kathleen Turner.** The lobby features the critically acclaimed 44 Restaurant, (212-944-8844) a round bar inspired by **Ernest Hemingway's** favorite bar at the Ritz in Paris, and space age–style rest rooms a local paper recently labeled Manhattan's "most appealing."

···**A**···

row of rock groupies was patiently waiting by the elevator hoping to be picked over by members of **Guns N' Roses,** *the rock group occupying suites in the Royalton Hotel. Meanwhile, group member* **Slash** *was busy throwing up on the Hemingway-inspired bar. Talk about having a fun evening!*

··

The final stop on this tour is a skyscraper that has been the symbol of New York City since its completion in 1931, the Empire State Building. To reach the 102-story structure from the Royalton Hotel, walk east along 54th Street, turn right at 5th Avenue, and head south—ten minutes on foot or five minutes by bus, or take a two-dollar taxi ride. Your destination is 350 5th Avenue,[30] at the southwest corner of 34th Street. Careful crossing the road, since I'm reminded of **Irene Dunne** being hit by a bus while running across 34th Street to meet **Charles Boyer** in the film *Love Affair* (1939).

This sleek grayish-toned New York landmark, which for more than forty years was the world's tallest building, entered into legend with the 1933 release of the film *King Kong.* A lovestruck gorilla perches himself atop the Empire State Building and proceeds to swat attacking planes. Fiction became fact in 1945 when a plane crashed into the skyscraper, killing fourteen people. Films *On the Town* (1949) and *An Affair to Remember* (1957) also featured the Empire State Building. For a spectacular view of the city and the rivers and bridges, take the elevator to the two observation decks, open between 9:30 A.M. and midnight.

As you leave the Empire State Building, you'll find access to buses and subways that will whisk you throughout the Big Apple. Crosstown buses are on 34th Street, and if you head one block west to the Avenue of the Americas, the B, Q, N, or R trains are at your disposal.

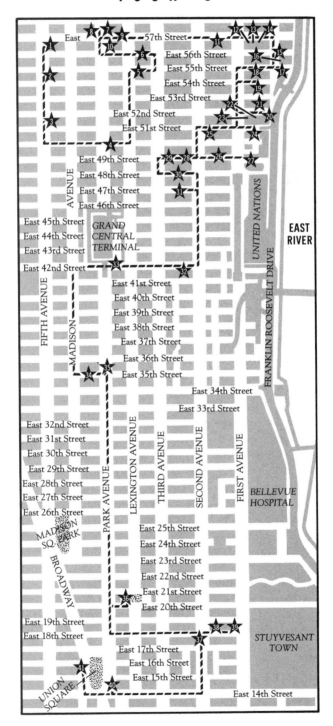

East 57th Street
East 56th Street
East 55th Street
East 54th Street
East 53rd Street
East 52nd Street
East 51st Street
East 49th Street
East 48th Street
East 47th Street
East 46th Street
East 45th Street
East 44th Street
East 43rd Street
East 42nd Street
East 41st Street
East 40th Street
East 39th Street
East 38th Street
East 37th Street
East 36th Street
East 35th Street
East 34th Street
East 33rd Street
East 32nd Street
East 31st Street
East 30th Street
East 29th Street
East 28th Street
East 27th Street
East 26th Street
East 25th Street
East 24th Street
East 23rd Street
East 22nd Street
East 21st Street
East 20th Street
East 19th Street
East 18th Street
East 17th Street
East 16th Street
East 15th Street
East 14th Street

FIFTH AVENUE
MADISON AVENUE
PARK AVENUE
LEXINGTON AVENUE
THIRD AVENUE
SECOND AVENUE
FIRST AVENUE
BROADWAY

GRAND CENTRAL TERMINAL
MADISON SQ. PARK
UNION SQUARE

UNITED NATIONS
FRANKLIN ROOSEVELT DRIVE
EAST RIVER
BELLEVUE HOSPITAL
STUYVESANT TOWN

East

STAR SEARCH

MIDTOWN EAST

T O P ★ 10 ★ T E N

STARS IN THE AREA

Johnny Carson ☆ Richard Chamberlain ☆ Phil Collins ☆ Katharine Hepburn ☆ Sophia Loren ☆ Kelly McGillis ☆ Julia Roberts ☆ Frank Sinatra ☆ Stevie Wonder ☆ Pia Zadora

NUMBER	ADDRESS	NAME
1	721 5th Avenue	**Donald Trump**
		Sophia Loren
		Pia Zadora
		Johnny Carson
		Dick Clark
		Steven Spielberg
		Paul Anka
		Martina Navratilova
		Fay Wray
		Andrew Lloyd Weber
		Susan Saint James
		I'll Take Manhattan
2	2 East 55th Street	**Marlene Dietrich** (deceased)
		Rex Harrison (deceased)
		Ernest Hemingway (deceased)
		Hannah and Her Sisters
		Radio Days
		Taxi Driver
3	641 5th Avenue	**Adnan Khashoggi**
		Laura Branigan
		Patti Austin
4	100 East 50th Street	**Frank Sinatra**
		Spencer Tracy (deceased)
		Gregory Peck
		Cole Porter (deceased)
		Marilyn Monroe (deceased)
5	135 East 55th Street	**Billy Idol**
6	146 East 56th Street	**David Rockefeller**
7	465 Park Avenue	**Norman Lear**
		Greta Garbo (deceased)
		Arlene Francis
		William Randolph Hearst (deceased)
		Marion Davies (deceased)
		Neil Simon

8	470 Park Avenue	Darren McGavin
9	117 East 57th Street	Eric Clapton Buck Henry
10	110 East 57th Street	Phil Collins
11	322 East 57th Street	Kathie Lee Gifford Frank Gifford
12	430 East 57th Street	Lillian Gish (deceased)
13	444 East 57th Street	Bill Blass Marilyn Monroe (deceased)
14	447 East 57th Street	Bobby Short
15	25 Sutton Place	Charlotte Ford
16	36 Sutton Place	*How to Marry a Millionaire*
17	50 Sutton Place	Maureen O'Hara
18	404 East 55th Street	Noel Coward (deceased)
19	405 East 54th Street	Van Johnson
20	450 East 52nd Street	Greta Garbo (deceased) Rex Harrison (deceased)
21	435 East 52nd Street	Henry Kissinger
22	434 East 52nd Street	Humphrey Bogart (deceased)
23	400 East 52nd Street	Shirley MacLaine
24	433 East 51st Street	Richard Chamberlain
25	300 East 51st Street	Joe Namath
26	342 East 49th Street	Michael Cimino
27	870 United Nations Plaza	Dina Merrill Truman Capote (deceased)
28	244 East 49th Street	Katharine Hepburn
29	246 East 49th Street	Stephen Sondheim
30	228 East 48th Street	Kurt Vonnegut, Jr.
31	240 East 47th Street	Rita Moreno
32	220 East 42nd Street	*Superman*
33	Grand Central Terminal (42nd Street and Lexington Avenue)	*The Prince of Tides* *North by Northwest* *The Cotton Club*
34	20 East 35th Street	Vivian Blaine
35	30 Park Avenue	Jackie Mason
36	7 Gramercy Park West	Julia Roberts
37	305 Second Avenue	Judd Nelson David Lee Roth Wesley Snipes
38	325 East 18th Street	Stevie Wonder
39	327 East 18th Street	Wynton Marsalis
40	One Irving Place	Kelly McGillis
41	31 Union Square West	Elizabeth Ashley

Legendary actress **Katharine Hepburn's** upper-class Connect-
icut background, well-bred manners, and desire to maintain
a low-key lifestyle are indicative of the many celebrities hav-

ing homes in this area. **Greta Garbo** created curiosity among fans and journalists with her elusiveness. Ritzy Midtown East attracts celebrities with the cash resources necessary to lead a proper existence in one of the most expensive areas of Manhattan. Since prominent socialites exercise a strong hold on may of the luxurious complexes, proper connections can be essential to becoming part of this well-established community.

The convenience and exclusivity of the area have made it a perfect home for many millionaires and even a few billionaires. Banker **David Rockefeller** resides here. So does **Adnan Khashoggi,** who is considered to be one of the richest men in the world.

"Hairdressers to the Stars" must believe that healthy competition leads to healthy hair and healthy profits, since the majority of these posh shops are located in Midtown East. As **Kenneth,** owner of Kenneth Beauty Salon in the elegant Waldorf-Astoria Hotel, will attest, the trend is to locate in one of the neighborhood's chic department stores or classy hotels. You will also notice that many of New York's most expensive restaurants are sprinkled throughout the area. I guess the thinking is, Where better to show off the new do than at an intimate eating establishment visited with one's agent, producer, or casting director?

Our tour will commence at the star-studded Trump Tower, 721 5th Avenue, and will culminate at the home of actress **Elizabeth Ashley,** who resides at 31 Union Square West. The area to be covered is bounded by 5th Avenue on the west, the East River on the east, 14th on the south, and 58th Street on the north.

Starting Address:	**Corner of 57th Street and 5th Avenue**
Length of Tour:	**2 Hours, 45 Minutes**
Best Starting Time:	**11:00 A.M. or 2:00 P.M.**
Subway:	**E, F, N, or R to 5th Avenue**
Bus:	**1, 57, or 58**
Bring Along:	**A few credit cards (one might not be enough) and a camera— and dress fashionably so you blend in**

☆ THE TOUR

Trump Tower, 721 5th Avenue,① with its waterfall and its six-story pink marble atrium, is jam-packed with stars seeking a sleek, modern-looking home. A residence here can garner a celebrity much publicity, for the glitzy glass tower is one of New York's leading tourist attractions. To reach Trump Tower, head from your bus or subway stop to the fashionable and exclusive corner of 5th Avenue and 57th Street. If coming from 5th Avenue and 60th Street (N or R train), head sough on 5th Avenue three blocks. The E or F train will take you to 5th and 53rd, from which you will walk five blocks north on 5th Avenue.

The top three floors of this elegant monument are home to the tower's namesake, **Donald Trump,** famed deal-maker and star of his own never-ending one-man show. The Donald's residence, with elegant furnishings, including twenty-seven hand-crafted marble columns, is definitely fit for a king.

Trump Tower, 721 Fifth Avenue

Judith Krantz's television miniseries *I'll Take Manhattan,* based on her book of that name, was filmed at Trump Tower. Donald appeared in the film, cast as his favorite person: himself. He returns to the silver screen in the same role when **Macaulay Culkin** bumps into him at the Plaza Hotel in *Home Alone 2* (1992). Considering the precarious state of his once-mighty finances, Donald may soon be dependent on his movie earnings to keep his yacht stocked with caviar.

··· **D**onald Trump *may soon be replaced on the dating scene by his ten-year-old daughter,* **Ivanka.** *The stunning child has been spotted window-shopping in the vicinity of Trump Tower with* Home Alone *star* **Macaulay Culkin.**

Sensuously beautiful actress **Sophia Loren,** who resides at Trump Tower, has a tough time blending into the constant rush of humanity that encircles the building. The usual sun-

glasses and kerchief do little to conceal her seductive facial features
and voluptuous figure from stargazers. The sexy **Pia Zadora** also lives
at 721 5th Avenue, but how long
that will last, I have no idea. She
complains of landlord Donald
Trump's arrogance and he jokes
about her lack of talent.

The original home of NBC's
"Tonight Show" in Rockefeller
Plaza is only minutes from **Johnny
Carson's** home in Trump Tower.
Perhaps Johnny will spend more

Sophia Loren

time in the Big Apple now that he's left the show he hosted
for thirty years. He'll likely continue to be as active as his

Pia Zadora

Trump Tower neighbor, the
timeless **Dick Clark,** whose
many years hosting TV's
"American Bandstand" have
been followed by his production of many television specials.

Another Trump Tower res-
ident is the influential film director **Steven Spielberg,** called
the "Magician of the Movies"
by *Time* magazine in its 1985

cover story on him. Singer-
composer **Paul Anka** lives here,
as does eight-time Wimble-
don champion **Martina Navratilova,** the top money earner in
tennis history, male or female.

Johnny Carson

··· ❙ ·······································
        f an automobile pulls up to Trump Tower with XCZECH on
the license plate, say hello to **Martina Navratilova.** *This tennis
great still remembers her Czechoslovakian birthplace, even though
she's now an American citizen.*

···

Fay Wray will always be remembered as the frightened girl
clutched tenderly by an infatuated giant-sized gorilla as he
climbed the Empire State Building in the movie *King Kong*

(1933). Fay's home in Trump Tower is within sight of the 102-story landmark that marks the height of her career.

Trump Tower is also home to **Andrew Lloyd Webber,** composer of a slew of Broadway hits. His neighbor at this fashionable address is actress **Susan Saint James,** costar of TV's "Kate and Allie."

When **Bernadette Peters, Lily Tomlin, Tina Sinatra,** and **Margaux Hemingway** are spotted in Trump Tower, they're probably heading to Pierre Michel Coiffeur. **Pierre Michel** is the hairstylist to many well-known celebrities.

.. **T** *..*

he former queen of Trump Tower, Donald's ex-wife, **Ivana,** *will spare no expense in nailing her next husband. The blond socialite spends close to $4,000 yearly on manicuring her inch-long fingernails. Whatever happened to the five-dollar manicure?*

..

Tiffany & Co.

Donald Trump chose to build his star-studded Trump Tower next door to where **Audrey Hepburn** had her ten-dollar shopping spree in the film *Breakfast at Tiffany's* (1961). Tiffany & Co., 727 5th Avenue, at the corner of 57th Street, attracts celebrities in search of that perfect melon-sized diamond. Remember, if you have to ask the price, you're in the wrong place. Some of the rich and famous, including Mr. Trump, prefer buying their ladies gems in the more intimate and personal setting Harry Winston, one block south at 718 5th Avenue, offers.

Celebrities without permanent New York homes enjoy staying at the newly renovated St. Regis Hotel, 2 East 55th Street. ② The hotel is a two-block walk from Trump Tower, down 5th Avenue to 55th Street. **Marlene Dietrich, Rex Harrison,** and **Ernest Hemingway** all resided on a long-term basis in this stately hotel, built in 1904 by **Colonel John Jacob Astor.** Cabbie **Robert De Niro** picked up an apologetic **Cybill Shepherd** at the St. Regis Hotel in the film *Taxi Driver* (1976). **Woody Allen** used the interior of the hotel extensively in

Hannah and Her Sisters (1986) and *Radio Days* (1987). Continue south on 5th Avenue.

A number of restaurants along 5th Avenue are ideal for stargazing. Bice, 7 East 54th Street (212-688-1999), is excellent for spotting magazine editors and fashion designers, as well as actors like **Dustin Hoffman** and **Michael Caine.** Lunch is the ideal time for celebrity watching and reservations are a must at this airy Italian eatery.

During lunchtime at La Grenouille, 3 East 52nd Street (212-752-1495), the front tables are reserved for the likes of

The St. Regis Hotel
2 E. 55th Street

Henry Kissinger, Oscar de la Renta, Liz Smith, and **Ivana Trump.** This charming restaurant is lavishly designed, with prices appropriately extravagant. Walk east on 52nd Street, crossing Park Avenue, to arrive at our next location.

One of Manhattan's two most celebrity-studded spots for lunch is The Four Seasons, 99 East 52nd Street (212-754-9494). (The Russian Tea Room is the other.) The Grill Room at The Four Seasons is territory set aside for the rich and famous, such as **Elton John, Bill Blass,** and **Barry Diller.** Food in this thirty-year-old restaurant is always delicious, the service perfect, and the tab steep. Double back on 52nd Street a couple of blocks to our next adventure, on the southeast corner of 5th Avenue, at the former Morton F. Plant Mansion, now an exquisite jewelry store.

Harry Winston, 718 Fifth Avenue

After lunching, many stars, including **Elizabeth Taylor, Elton John,** and **Eddie Murphy,** stop in at Cartier at 653 5th Avenue for desert. Even on a slow day for celebrity watching, wandering through this celebrated jewelry store is a treat.

... **E** ....
ddie Murphy must have thought there was a "blue light special" on when he and five bodyguards grabbed twos and threes of each item at Cartier. This last-minute Christmas shopping spree probably used up his salary from the movie—Boomerang (1992)—*he'd been filming all around town.*
....

Continue south on 5th Avenue to 51st Street and turn left. Just off the corner, on the north side of the road, is the entrance to our next stop. The mystique of Olympic Tower, 641 5th Avenue,③ has long attracted many celebrities. Its aura originated with its initial owner, shipping king **Aristotle Onassis,** who was married to **Jackie Kennedy Onassis** when the black boxlike glass structure was unveiled in 1974. One of the richest men in the world, billionaire **Adnan Khashoggi,** has a home in the Olympic Tower. The rooms in Adnan's residence are so large that even Donald Trump was impressed, calling the living room the largest he'd "ever witnessed."

... **M** ....
ost American men dream of being a sports hero, having a billion dollars, and being married to more than one woman at the same time. **Adnan Khashoggi** *has two out of three. The Saudi billionaire enjoys the companionship of two radiant wives:* **Shahpari,** *an Iranian, and* **Lamia,** *a native of Italy.*
....

The amenities the Olympic Tower offers include a wine cellar, a health club, and a stock-quotation board. Celebrities such as pop vocalist **Laura Branigan** enjoy residing in a building so comfortably appointed. Soul singer **Patti Austin,** whose stage debut was at the ripe young age of three at New York's Apollo Theater, has her fashionable home in the Olympic Tower. Also in the building resides Emmy Award–winning newscaster **Tom Jarriel.** Next stop on the tour is New York's grandest hotel, occupied by the city's grand master and singer of the immortal song "New York, New York." You arrive there by heading one block south on 5th Avenue to 50th Street, turning left, and walking two blocks east to the southeast corner of Park Avenue and 50th Street.

Frank Sinatra must have seen how exuberant **Ginger Rogers** appeared in the movie *Weekend at the Waldorf* (1945). Maybe the film led the "Chairman of the Board" to acquire a residence suite in the hotel as his Big Apple center of operations. The preeminent star has his home at 100 East 50th Street④ in the grandly decorated, discreetly located residence tower of the Waldorf-Astoria Hotel.

When *Frank Sinatra says he's throwing a party, expect two. After his star-studded bash for mayoral candidate* **Andrew Stein,** *Frank and his wife,* **Barbara,** *invited* **Liza Minnelli** *and* **Shirley MacLaine,** *among others, back to his luxurious Waldorf-Astoria residence to continue the festivities.*

Frank Sinatra

*The Waldorf Astoria Hotel-Towers
100 E. 50th Street*

Former residents of the tower section in this world-famous hotel have included acting greats **Spencer Tracy, Cole Porter, Gregory Peck** and movie goddess **Marilyn Monroe.** Hidden away from the hotel's main entrance, the tower has its own lobby and concierge service. Long-term leases can be negotiated, starting from the nightly rate of a bit less than $2,000 per suite.

The Waldorf-Astoria Hotel and its Art Deco lobby have been featured in numerous films. **Woody Allen** has taken advantage of the hotel's glamorous facade in a few of his films. The hotel also appeared in *The Out-of-Towners* (1970) *with* **Jack Lemmon** and *My Favorite Year* (1982), starring **Peter O'Toole.**

The original Waldorf-Astoria Hotel, which this one replaced in 1931, was located where the Empire State Building now stands. The first structure was the Hotel Waldorf, built by **William Waldorf Astor** in 1893 next door to the home of his socialite aunt **Mrs. William Astor** as a vindictive practical joke. The aunt got her revenge, however: She soon relocated and replaced her home with the Astoria Hotel. Eventually, the two hotels combined to form the first Waldorf-Astoria Hotel, predecessor to the current structure at Park Avenue near 50th Street.

The Waldorf-Astoria now hosts Kenneth Beauty Salon, whose regulars include **Joan Rivers, Lauren Bacall, Glenn Close, Sigourney Weaver,** and **Angie Dickinson.** They love being pampered by **Kenneth,** who first achieved fame with client **Jacqueline Kennedy's** bouffant hairdo in the 1960s. Continue east on 50th half a block past Lexington Avenue.

Almost any night is a stargazer's delight at New York's hottest supperclub, Tatou (212-753-1144), down the block at 151 East 50th Street. **Prince, Diana Ross, Isabella Rossellini, Sophia Loren, Eddie Murphy,** and **Richard Gere** with his wife, **Cindy Crawford,** among others, have checked out the scene. If you enjoy dancing and dining in a setting modeled after an old Southern opera house, Tatou is for you. We now turn around and walk west on 50th Street to Lexington Avenue, turn right, head five blocks north, and walk east on 55th Street.

Between 3rd and Lexington avenues, at 135 East 55th Street, ⑤ is the home of a sensual pop icon, guitarist **Billy Idol.** This young punk rocker is only one of a growing colony of rock stars taking advantage of New York's inspirational energies. To reach our next stop, head east a short distance on 55th Street.

Woody Allen plays his clarinet on Monday nights at Michael's Pub, 211 East 55th Street (212-758-2272). Woody has been appearing at this cozy club for over twenty years.

Go west on 55th Street to 3rd Avenue, turn right, and head north one block to 56th Street. There we turn left and walk a block to our next location. One forty-six East 56th Street⑥ is the home of wealthy banker **David Rockefeller.** David and the rest of the Rockefeller family have directed much of their enormous fortune toward philanthropic causes. They built Rockefeller Center, although the complex has since passed out of the family's hands. Continue walking west on 56th Street to Park Avenue and turn right. Up one block is our next stop.

The Ritz Towers, 465 Park Avenue,⑦ at the corner of 57th Street, is an elegant building that is home to writer, director, and producer **Norman Lear.** Norman has a lavish residence in this forty-two-story apartment-hotel that was once home to fabled actress **Greta Garbo.** Also in the building resides **Arlene Francis,** the actress and popular radio and television panelist. **William Randolph Hearst** owned the Ritz Towers from 1928 till 1938 and maintained a magnificent home there with his mistress, actress **Marion Davies.** He sold the building when his publishing empire began to crumble.

Bronx-born playwright **Neil Simon** is another resident of this comfortable complex. The most commercially successful playwright in American history, Neil owes much of his inspiration to his New York upbringing. He is one of the most succesful playwrights in the history of American theater.

Across the street, at 470 Park Avenue,⑧ resides versatile actor **Darren McGavin.** Darren, who was trained in the renowned Actors Studio, is as comfortable playing a shining hero as he is a ruthless villain. Next we head back to 57th Street, turn left, and stoll eastward.

Tatou, 151 E. 50th Street

Rock-and-roll stars choose New York City as their home base so often because of its incomparable musical facilities, its trend-setting clubs, and its energetic creative atmosphere. Guitarist **Eric Clapton** has his home in the heart of Manhattan, at 117 East 57th Street.⑨ Also in the building resides noted actor and screenwriter **Buck Henry,** best known for his collaboration on the script of the hit film *The Graduate* (1967).

··· **B**··

    Buck Henry *formed the Society for Indecency to Naked Animals and appeared on TV talk shows to promote the link between the "nudity of animals and the moral decline of man." This humorous hoax helped launch his career.*

··

Phil Collins

Across the street, at 110 East 57th Street⑩ is the home of rock and roller **Phil Collins.** Phil enjoys acting and singing equally and tries to balance his two careers as best he can.

A few shrewd New York realtors not only sell the stars exclusive Manhattan homes; they also socialize, vacation, and party with them. Realtor **Linda Stein,** of Douglas Elliman Realty, 575 Madison Avenue, has a client list that includes **Madonna, Elton John, Billy Joel, La Toya Jackson, Andrew Lloyd Webber, Sylvester Stallone,** and **Bruce Willis.** She recently brokered a deal that put Bruce and his wife, **Demi Moore,** in a $10 million triplex at the San Remo on Central Park West. Linda's abilities at pampering and sheltering superstars have helped her become one of a select handful of "Realtors to the Stars." Don't stray from the tour to call on her unless you're seeking your multimillion-dollar dreamhouse. Her office can be reached by heading west on 57th Street, making a left onto Madison Avenue, and walking south one and a half blocks. After exiting Linda's office, walk back up Madison Avenue, turn right, and head three blocks east to the corner of 3rd Avenue.

Now might be an excellent time to rest your weary legs.

Check out the Healthy Deli (212-688-5757) at 954 Third Avenue, just north of 57th Street. You'll go crazy trying to select from the healthy and varied dishes artfully displayed in a glass cooler. Look for a star lunching on the delicious Caesar salad as he or she makes ready for another entertainment-industry conquest. After a healthy snack, get back on track by turning left onto 57th Street and strolling east a block and a half.

Kathie Lee Gifford and her husband, **Frank,** have their home at 322 East 57th Street,[11] Kathie is cohost of the highly rated daytime talk show, "Live with Regis and Kathie Lee," which is taped in Manhattan. She and husband spend many hours involved in charitable organizations like the Special Olympics, a natural for Frank, star commentator on "Monday Night Football" and former halfback for the New York Giants. Despite their many activities, however, the couple always finds quality time to devote to America's most talked about baby, their son, **Cody.** Continue east on 57th Street, crossing 1st Avenue.

Four thirty East 57th Street[12] was the residence of the First Lady of the Silent Screen, **Lillian Gish.** Lillian continued to thrill audiences with powerful performances in recent films, which included *Sweet Liberty* (1986) with **Alan Alda** and *The Whales of August* (1987), which costarred **Bette Davis** right up until her death in February 1993 at the age of 99.

Next door, at 444 East 57th Street[13] is the present home of designer **Bill Blass** and the former home of **Marilyn Monroe.** Marilyn lived in this posh building on the thirteenth floor, first with her then husband, playwright **Arthur Miller,** and later alone, after the couple divorced, until her death in 1962.

··· **M** ··
arilyn Monroe's residence was almost like a mood ring in the way it reflected her highs and lows. When life was grand, much time was spent at home cooking and decorating, but in troubled times Marilyn's kitchen became bare and her furnishings filthy.
··

Across the street, at 447 East 57th Street,[14] is the home of celebrated pianist **Bobby Short.** Reserve a table to see him perform in the Carlyle Hotel's Cafe Carlyle, where he appears regularly. Walk east along 57th Street to Sutton Place South as you notice the magnificent view of the East River. Then turn right and head south a block.

Marilyn Monroe

Sutton Place, named after nineteenth-century land developer **Effingham B. Sutton,** is a relaxed and pleasant area lined
with elegant town houses and residential complexes. Enjoy
the beautiful view of the East River and the Queensboro (Fifty-
ninth Street) Bridge.

Marilyn Monroe must have decided while on the set of the
film *How to Marry a Mlilionaire* (1953), shot on location at 36
Sutton Place South,[16] to reside in this posh neighborhood
one day. She and her costars **Lauren Bacall** and **Betty Grable**
used this fashionable building as bait to trap their wealthy
prey. Two years later, actress **Joan Crawford** moved into an
eight-room residence at this same address. Also in this fashionable area, in a modern high rise across the street at 25
Sutton Place South,[15] resides New York socialite **Charlotte
Ford.** Continue south.

Fifty Sutton Place South[17] is the home of beautiful leading
lady **Maureen O'Hara.** This redheaded native of Ireland
worked at Macy's in the 1947 Christmas classic, *Miracle on
34th Street.*

From Sutton Place South, take 55th Street west to 1st
Avenue for our next stop. Just off the corner of 1st Avenue
is the former home of playwright **Noel Coward** at 404 East
55th Street,[18] where he lived part of the time until his death
in 1973. One block south, at 405 East 54th Street[19] lovable,
freckled-faced actor **Van Johnson,** who began his career by
way of Broadway chorus lines, resides in a spacious home with
a magnificent view of the bridge. To reach our next residence
building, walk two blocks south on 1st Avenue, turn left, and
head east one block.

The Campanile, which at 450 East 52nd Street[20] is tucked
away on a cul-de-sac, reflects the very private superstars who
choose it as home. For many years, it was home both to **Greta**

Garbo and **Rex Harrison,** both of whom passed away in 1990. Sir Rex, the "gentleman actor," thrilled Broadway and movie audiences with his Professor Henry Higgins character in *My Fair Lady*, but he preferred a private lifestyle offstage. "I vant to be alone" Garbo's credo, kept her secluded behind the leaded glass windows in her elegant seven-room residence. She did venture out—but usually covered by a trench coat, sunglasses, and hat.

We now head to the home of one of America's most popular secretaries of state by changing direction and strolling a few doors west down 52nd Street. Foreign-affairs guru **Henry Kissinger** has become a serious Manhattan socialite, using his masterly diplomatic skills to balance his extraordinary volume of dinner invitations. Henry resides in the twenty-six-story River House at 435 East 52nd Street.[21] This luxurious building is across from 434 East 52nd Street,[22] once home to New York–born acting great **Humphrey Bogart.** Head back along 52nd Street to 1st Avenue.

Oscar-winning actress **Shirley MacLaine** lives in a modern building at 400 East 52nd Street.[23] I hope that Shirley, who has maintained as many as eight dwellings at one time, didn't go "out on a limb" when adding this home to her holdings. Continue south on 1st Avenue one block and make a left, heading east on 51st Street.

• • • **S**hirley *MacLaine denies using her psychic skills when suggesting* **Carol Haney** *"break a leg," a traditional theatric expression. Still, Carol did just that. Shirley replaced the injured star, getting not only a starring role in Broadway's* Pajama Game *but also the big break she needed to launch what became a phenomenally successful career.*

• •

433 E. 51st Street

Actor **Richard Chamberlain,** champion of the miniseries, resides at 433 East 51st Street,[24] which faces Beekman Place. This tranquil, isolated area with its eclectic mix of buildings has always attracted prominent New Yorkers. Turn around and head west on 51st Street to the corner of 2nd Avenue.

Pro football Hall of Famer and

current TV commentator **"Broadway" Joe Namath** resides in a modern high rise at 300 East 51st Street.[25] If you head south two blocks on 2nd Avenue and turn left on 49th Street, you'll arrive at 342 East 49th Street[26] the home of screenwriter and director **Michael Cimino.**

Continue walking east on 49th Street a short distance to arrive at 870 United Nationas Plaza,[27] a glittering glass tower that is home to attractive blond actress **Dina Merrill,** who is the youngest daughter of Manhattan socialite **Marjorie Merriweather Post.** That impressive lineage helped groom her for the aristocratic characters she has convincingly portrayed. Built in 1966, the building has been home to a number of celebrities, including author **Truman Capote,** who lived in a spacious twenty-second-floor suite till his death in 1984. To reach the home of the next star on the tour, head back on 49th Street west one and a half blocks, until you cross 2nd Avenue.

Turtle Bay could easily be labeled "Celebrity Town Houses," in that it comprises two streets of charming picturesque buildings housing the most famous of stars. The town houses, each with its own private garden, encompass 48th and 49th streets between 2nd and 3rd avenues. Legend has it that the origin of the area's name lies in the many turtles that filled the shores of the bay, atop which is now the United Nations complex. Legendary actress **Katharine Hepburn** has lived at 244 East 49th Street[28] in the heart of Turtle Bay for over fifty years. Her four-story town house, for which she paid just $27,500 in 1937, is fronted by black wrought-iron gates that protect this very private four-time Academy Award–winning actress from autograph hounds.

... **K**atharine Hepburn *glared into her fireplace and threatened one day to break through into* **Stephen Sondheim's** *attached dwelling and surprise him with a visit. A smiling mutual friend of both Katharine and myself offered to go home and change into something more appropriate for digging, but Katharine never followed through on her plan. Above her fireplace is a beautiful painting of Spence (Katharine's nickname for* **Spencer Tracy***), the love of her life.*

Next door to Katharine resides New York–born **Stephen Sondheim,** who has composed scores and written lyrics for some of the most popular film and stage productions in history. Stephen

Katharine Hepburn

resides in a brownstone at 246 East 49th Street.[29] Around
the corner, south one block, between 2nd and 3rd Avenues,
at 230 East 48th Street (still in Turtle Bay) lives the "incomparable" **Hildegarde.** For over fifty years, this flamboyant singer
has dazzled audiences. Her trademark handkerchief and long
gloves have been around so long that the government finally
cleaned a set and placed it in the Smithsonian. Next door to
Hildegarde, at 228 East 48th Street,[30] resides author **Kurt
Vonnegut, Jr.** Kurt is often seen chatting with area neighbors.

Another block south, at 240 East 47th Street,[31] reached
by taking 2nd Avenue to 47th Street and turning right, lives
singer and dancer **Rita Moreno.** At the tender age of thirteen,
Rita made her Broadway debut, going on to star in many
Broadway productions. Return to 2nd Avenue and head south
five blocks to the southwest corner of 42nd Street.

The Man of Steel flew to the Daily News Building at 220
East 42nd Street,[32] but you'll have to walk the ten minutes
there. The movie *Superman,* starring Gothamite **Christopher
Reeve,** was partly filmed in 1978 in this remarkable 1930 slab
building that masqueraded as the offices of the *Daily Planet.*

If you continue west a few blocks on 42nd Street, you arrive
at Grand Central Terminal,[33] the architectural heart of New
York City. (Grand Central Station, the name most often used
to denote the structure, is actually the name of the post office
up the block.) This massive railroad station on 42nd Street
between Lexington and Park avenues was where **Nick Nolte**

waved good-bye to **Barbra Streisand's** son in the movie *The Prince of Tides* (1991). Among other films shot on location in Grand Central are **Alfred Hitchcock's** *North by Northwest* (1959) and **Francis Ford Coppola's** *The Cotton Club* (1984).

Next, walk west one block to Madison Avenue, turn left, head south seven blocks to 35th Street, and turn left again. A few doors east is 20 East 35th Street,㉞ home of actress **Vivian Blaine.** At seventy-two, Vivian is still that warm and lively lady who thrilled Broadway audiences for years in *Guys and Dolls.* A short walk east on 35th Street brings us to the home of comic **Jackie Mason,** who resides at 30 Park Avenue. ㉟ Jackie's had a rocky career but is back on top since his own Broadway show. He relishes his newfound popularity and loves to schmooze with autograph seekers. South on Park Avenue fifteen short blocks to 7 Gramery Park West㊱ brings us to the home of "Pretty Woman" **Julia Roberts** who, after stints in L.A. and Ireland, has chosen to reside in the Big Apple. Continue down to 18th Street and three lengthy blocks east.

... **R**ecently *Vivian Blaine performed at home in concert for her dog,* **Ade** *(named after Adelaide, Vivian's character in* Guys and Dolls)*, in tandem with her pet groomer. The pooch joined in for the final chorus.*

Rutherford Place, 305 Second Avenue,㊲ once the largest maternity hospital in the United States, has been renovated and converted into an extremely attractive residence complex. R. H. Robertson, one of the period's most prolific and distinguished architects, designed this magnificent structure (built in 1902). High ceilings and multi-level dwelling units are features that have lured many celebrities to set up home here. Handsome young actor **Judd Nelson** has his residence in Rutherford Place, as does talented actor **Wesley Snipes.** Coincidentally, Judd and Wesley recently appeared together in the film *New Jack City* (1991). Rock star **David Lee Roth** also resides in the complex. Next, walk a few doors further east on 18th Street.

Stevie Wonder, who has astounded music lovers with a constant flow of Grammy Award–winning songs lives in a town house at 325 East 18th Street.㊳ Fittingly, his neighbor, at 327 East 18th Street㊳ is the young influential jaza trumpeter **Wynton Marsalis,** who has won Grammys for both jazz and classical recordings.

... **W**...
hile I was researching some of the famous stars residing in the neighborhood, a very beautiful **Mrs. Wynton Marsalis** *described with excitement how popular the area has become. This modest lady spoke of the many stars living nearby, purposely omitting mention of her superstar hubby.*

....

We next head west to 2nd Avenue, turn left, walk south to 14th Street, turn right, and stroll a few block west. Our destination is 126 East 14th Street, a multimillion-dollar nightclub called the Palladium, which attracts the most famous of stars. On one recent visit, **Madonna** had a few too many and wound up behind the bar serving drinks. Before too much longer, the "Material Girl" was on top of the bar, voguing the night away. That same bar was where **Michael J. Fox** ordered a rum and Coke in the film *Bright Lights, Big City* (1988). Michael's coke came in powdered, not liquid, form.

Across 14th Street, and a few buildings west, at One Irving Place, ⑩ heartthrob **Kelly McGillis** lives in the modern Zeckendorf Towers. As a teenager, Kelly was consumed by acting and moved to New York to attend Juilliard School of Drama. Her neighbor, on the west side of Union Square Park, at 31 Union Square West, ⑪ is the versatile stage and screen actress **Elizabeth Ashley,** whose fiery presence helped her win a Tony for her work in *Take Her, She's Mine,* her very first Broadway production.

Elizabeth resides directly across from Union Square Park, which is a major stop for many of the subway trains connecting throughout the city.

TOUR 6

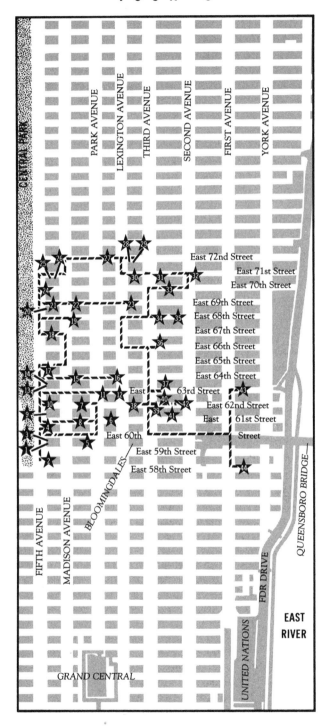

WALK OF FAME
UPPER EAST SIDE

T O P ★ T E N
STARS IN THE AREA

Carol Channing ☆ Bill Cosby ☆ Myrna Loy ☆ Elle MacPherson ☆ Liza Minnelli ☆ Dolly Parton ☆ Joan Rivers ☆ Diana Ross ☆ Brooke Shields ☆ Marlo Thomas

NUMBER	ADDRESS	NAME
1	781 5th Avenue	Diana Ross Francis Ford Coppola Danny Kaye (deceased)
2	767 5th Avenue	*Big*
3	785 5th Avenue	David Geffen
4	799 5th Avenue	Claire Trevor
5	502 Park Avenue	Richard Harris Robert Altman Ed Sullivan (deceased)
6	540 Park Avenue	Carol Channing
7	563 Park Avenue	John Irving
8	40 East 61st Street	Elle MacPherson
9	800 5th Avenue	Dolly Parton Pierre Cardin
10	1 East 62nd Street	Marlon Brando Joan Rivers
11	130 East 63rd Street	Baron R. de Rothschild
12	139 East 63rd Street	Sally Jessy Raphael
13	820 5th Avenue	Ann Getty
14	828 5th Avenue	Shere Hite Donna Summer
15	32 East 64th Street	Kitty Carlisle Hart
16	129 East 64th Street	Otto Preminger
17	834 5th Avenue	John DeLorean Carolyn Roehm Henry Kravis
18	16 East 67th Street	Bob Guccione
19	30 East 68th Street	Mary Stewart
20	875 5th Avenue	Marlo Thomas Phil Donahue

21	15 East 69th Street	**Fanny Brice** (deceased) **Ilie Nastase**
22	52 East 69th Street	**Jayne Mansfield** (deceased)
23	150 East 69th Street	**Liza Minnelli** **Doris Lilly** (deceased) **Howard Cosell**
24	2 East 70th Street	**Valentino** **Oscar de la Renta** **Joan Crawford** (deceased)
25	3 East 71st Street	**Bess Myerson**
26	18 East 71st Street	**Bill Cosby**
27	114 East 72nd Street	*Midnight Cowboy*
28	150 East 72nd Street	**Arlene Dahl**
29	160 East 72nd Street	**Joan Fontaine**
30	171 East 71st Street	*Breakfast at Tiffany's*
31	200 East 71st Street	**Louise Lasser**
32	300 East 71st Street	**Lana Cantrell**
33	211 East 70th Street	**Kaye Ballard** **Virginia Graham** **Sidney Poitier**
34	215 East 68th Street	**Arthur Miller** **Sammy Cahn** (deceased)
35	230 East 68th Street	**Morley Safer**
36	200 East 66th Street	**Imogene Coca** **Benny Goodman** (deceased) **Grace Kelly** (deceased)
37	212 East 63rd Street	**Francesco Scavullo**
38	165 East 62nd Street	**Brooke Shields**
39	200 East 62nd Street	**Peggy Cass**
40	201 East 62nd Street	**Rona Jaffe**
41	229 East 62nd Street	**David Brenner**
42	232 East 62nd Street	**Tom Wolfe**
43	425 East 63rd Street	**Myrna Loy**
44	425 East 58th Street	**Ginger Rogers**

The Upper East Side was designed to be the residential community of the rich and famous. Architects conceived and developers built lavish brick and limestone high rises all along 5th and Park avenues, as well as elegant town houses on the side streets. To feed the shopping fantasies of the residents, they added Madison Avenue, which was to be filled with discreet boutiques.

On this tour, we will pass the homes of some of the wealthiest celebrities in the world. Included are movie stars, rock-and-roll greats, award-winning directors, Manhattan socialites, acclaimed writers, and legendary clothing designers. As we crisscross the numbered streets, a visit to one of the many shops and restaurants that punctuate ritzy Madison Avenue might be a treat. While you gaze at the expensive window displays, remember that these shops cater to neighborhood residents—a situation that makes Madison fertile ground for stargazing.

Our starting point will be the home of singing sensation **Diana Ross,** who resides at 781 5th Avenue in the Sherry-Netherland Hotel. The tour will culminate at 425 East 58th Street, which is the residence of classic movie star **Ginger Rogers.** The area we will be covering is bounded by East 58th Street on the south, East 62nd Street on the north, 5th Avenue on the west, and the East River on the east.

Starting Address:	**5th Avenue at 59th Street**
Length of Tour:	**2 hours, 25 minutes**
Best Starting Time:	**11:00 A.M.**
Subway:	**N or R to Fifth Avenue**
Bus:	**1, 30, Q32, 57, or 58**
Bring Along:	**Credit Cards, sports jacket, camera, and a blanket in case you might enjoy relaxing in Central Park**

☆ THE TOUR

Only a few doors south of the N and R subway exit at the corner of 5th Avenue and 60th Street is that first stop on the tour. To reach the same location by the 57th Street bus, disembark at 5th Avenue and walk north two blocks to 59th Street.

The Sherry-Netherland, 781 Fifth Avenue

Fashionable 5th Avenue is where singer-actress **Diana Ross** makes her home. She lives at 781 5th Avenue,① in one of the supreme tower suites in the elegant Sherry-Netherland Hotel. Diana has given back much to her adopted hometown. This "Female Entertainer of the Century," as *Billboard* magazine called her, gave a free outdoor concert in Central Park for over a quarter of a million people and helped finance a playground near the concert site.

... **D**iana Ross *had her free Central Park concert televised in order to raise funds necessary to fulfill her long-sought dream of building a playground for the children of New York. Unfortunately, Diana's concert was marred by a torrential downpour and the cleanup soaked the city for most of the cash the event earned. Diana wouldn't let that shortfall rain on her parade, however, so she came through with the extra dollars needed to make her dream a reality.*

Diana Ross

Also residing in the Sherry-Netherland is New York–raised director **Francis Ford Coppola,** most noted for his *Godfather* films. Coppola's commute to work when filming his segment of *New York Stories* (1989) was an easy one since it was shot on location in his residence complex. Brooklyn–born comedian and film actor **Danny Kaye** was a fellow resident until his death. The hotel's imaginative architectural style, exquisite marble lobby, and romantic setting make it a much sought-after celebrity domicile.

.. **L***ooking for a bargain? Check out **Francis Ford Coppola's** Sherry-Netherland residence and make an offer he can't refuse on the asking price: $3 million. **Danny Kaye's** daughter **Dena** has put her late father's Sherry-Netherland two-bedroom home on the real estate market for $2.5 million. Maybe a two-for-one price is negotiable.*

Next door, at the southeast corner of 59th Street on the ground floor of the fifty-story glass and marble General Motors Building, is the most exciting toy store in the world, F. A. O. Schwartz. **Tom Hanks** danced on a giant keyboard in the film *Big*, shot in 1988 in this gigantic playland at 767 5th Avenue. ② Continue back up 5th Avenue, passing the many artists and musicians who line the wayside along the west side of the street.

F. A. O. Schwarz
767 Fifth Avenue

At 785 5th Avenue③ is the home of record mogul **David Geffen.** An avid New Yorker, David can be seen at many of the trendier restaurants in town. One afternoon while lunching at the Russian Tea Room, I was told that Mr. Geffen, dressed in jeans and running shoes, was turned away by a newly hired doorman. The entertainment power broker soon received a note of apology from restaurant management. Continue north on 5th Avenue.

The classiest hotel in Gotham is most definitely the Pierre, 799 5th Avenue. ④ With its elegantly adorned rooms and a nearly two-to-one staff-to-guest ratio, the hotel has become a favorite of celebrities like **Charles Bronson, Jimmy Stewart, Tom Jones,** and **Audrey Hepburn.** The Pierre's perfect view has inspired resident writers such as **Dashiell Hammett** (*The Thin Man* and *The Maltese Falcon*) and **John O'Hara** (*Pal Joey*). New York actress **Claire Trevor** is presently a resident of the Pierre. Much of her early career was spent typecast as a golden-hearted floozy, but her crowning moment came when she earned an Academy Award for the 1948 film *Key Largo*. Photos of that suspense thriller's leading man, **Humphrey Bogart,** are conspicuously placed about her antique-laden home.

The barbershop at the Pierre Hotel is where celebrities like **Al Pacino, Ryan O'Neal,** and **Luciano Pavarotti** meet to have their locks trimmed while they discuss their latest movie or concert deals. If you don't mind being clipped for thirty-five dollars, visit Gio's Barber Shop, 2 East 61st Street. Head back to 60th Street and turn left.

At 10 East 60th Street is a nightclub immortalized in movies and music, the Copacabana. In the forties and fifties, it reigned supreme as the preeminent place for celebrities to be seen. Gossip columnists like **Walter Winchell** worked the tables nightly. Headliners included **Frank Sinatra, Sammy Davis, Jr., Dean Martin** and **Jerry Lewis, Lena Horne,** and **Jimmy Durante.** Beware, there is a possibility the club may be moving to a new Manhattan location. Continue on 60th Street to Park Avenue and turn right.

The Copacabana,   *10 E. 60th Street*

... **F** ....

rank Sinatra *went looking for comedian and well-known imbiber* **Joe E. Lewis,** *who hadn't appeared for his 8:00 and 11:00 P.M. shows at the Copacabana. When he discovered his buddy plastered at a nearby bar, Frank told him, "You're on." "How am I doing?" responded the tipsy jokester. (The life story of Joe E. Lewis, who switched to comedy after his vocal cords were damaged in a mob attack, was the subject of the 1957 film* The Joker Is Wild. *He was portrayed by none other than his good friend Frank Sinatra.)*

....

Delmonico's is a thirty-two story building at 502 Park Avenue,⑤ which is home to Broadway and film star **Richard Harris.** The building, also the residence of director **Robert Altman,** at one time housed the late television variety-show host **Ed Sullivan.** Walk north on Park Avenue a couple of blocks to our next stop.

Carol Channing, the actress best remembered as Dolly Gallagher Levi in the play *Hello, Dolly!*—in which she appeared for over three thousand performances—resides at 540 Park Avenue.⑥ These days, she keeps busy creating children's records and appearing as a guest on numerous TV shows. A few doors north, at 563 Park Avenue⑦ is the home of **John Irving,** author of the novel *The World According to Garp.*

···**W**··
        hen **Carol Channing** *lunches at the Russian Tea Room,*
she brings her own food. She claims her concoction of a grassy
substance mixed with dried fish, prepared at home and placed on
the restaurant's fine china, helps her stay young and healthy.
···

Our next stop if the Manhattan home of stunning supermodel **Elle MacPherson,** who resides at 40 East 61st Street.⑧ Her home can be reached by heading west on 61st Street from Park Avenue toward 5th Avenue.

Down the block is Aureole, 34 East 61st Street (212-319-1660), an informal restaurant with prices not so casual. Chef **Charles Palmer** turns this elegant town house into a food lover's paradise that draws the likes of **Daryl Hannah, Goldie**

Elle MacPherson

Hawn, Dustin Hoffman, and **Matthew Broderick.** If you're so inclined, check on lunch reservations and hope for a cancellation. Continue west to 5th Avenue and turn right.

One-of-a-kind singer and actress **Dolly Parton** lives at 800 5th Avenue⑨ in a well-built thirty-three-story structure. Designers of the com-

Dolly Parton

plex, completed in 1978, wanted it to blend with the older
Pierre Hotel next door, so they gave the lower levels an elegant
limestone front. Another resident of the building is the classic
clothing designer **Pierre Cardin.**

··· **T**he doormen at 800 5th Avenue were very open in describing
*Ivana and Donald Trump, who lived there before they opened
their own Trump Tower. Donald came across as a decent gentleman
(somewhat thrifty!) and quite the ladies' man. Ivana, however,
was always pompous, so the building's staff were relieved when the
couple moved out.*

1 E. 62nd Street

Just off 5th Avenue, at 1 East
62nd Street,⑩ is the home of
comedienne and talk-show host
Joan Rivers. Born **Joan Molin-
sky** in Brooklyn, she started
out as a starving young comic
in New York's Greenwich Village, but her career soared after
her first appearance on the
"Tonight Show," which she
later guest-hosted. Today, Joan
has her own talk show, ap-
proppriately called the "Joan
Rivers Show," which is taped
in the Big Apple. Merchants
and restaurant owners in Joan's
neighborhood find her down-to-earth, a naturally funny
woman who's a generous tipper. **Marlon Brando** also has his
New York residence in this classic
building. Brando studied acting
under **Stella Adler** at the Actors
Studio which prepared him for the
stage role of Stanley Kowalski in
Tennessee Williams's *A Streetcar
Named Desire,* that catapulted him
to stardom. The complex was also
home to writer **Ernest Hemingway**
until a year before his death in
1961. We next head up 5th Avenue
to 63rd Street, turn right, and walk
a few blocks, crossing Park Avenue.

Joan Rivers

One thirty east 63rd Street[11] is the home of **Baron R. de Rothschild,** of the famed international family of bankers. His neighbor a few doors east is the warm and insightful talk-show host **Sally Jessy Raphael.** This stubborn lady, who was fired from eighteen broadcasting jobs before achieving stunning success in both radio and television, resides at 139 East 63rd Street.[12]

S
ally Jessy Raphael feels she's well suited to New York. New Yorkers are success-driven; so is she. Manhattan is a restaurant town; Sally is a restaurant person. New York is filled with theaters; she adores the theater. Her fantasy is to have time to enjoy all these delights.

B A R B I Z O N

The Barbizon Hotel, 140 East 63rd Street, is presently a very fashionable full-service hotel, but it was once a boardinghouse for aspiring actresses. Stars who once lived in this attractive redbrick building include **Liza Minnelli, Candice Bergen, Grace Kelly, Joan Crawford,** and **Cloris Leachman.** Walk west to 5th Avenue to arrive at our next residence.

Eight seventeen 5th Avenue is where **Richard Nixon** tried to purchase an apartment for $970,000. (His application was impeached by the condo board.) The former President instead purchased a nearby town house. At a twelve-story luxury complex across the street, at 820 5th Avenue,[13] New York socialite **Ann Getty** occupies the entire floor, which includes five bedrooms, six bathrooms, and seven servant's rooms.

Farther north, author and surveyor of sexuality **Shere Hite** has her home at 828 5th Avenue.[14] In the same classic building lives songstress **Donna Summer.** We next travel east on 64th Street a short distance.

Best known for her fact-finding on the once-popular television show "To Tell the Truth," **Kitty Carlisle Hart** resides at 32 East 64th Street.[15] The former actress and singer is involved in a wide range of public-service activities and has twice served as chairwoman of the New York Council of the Arts. Film director **Otto Preminger** lived two blocks farther east, off Lexington Avenue, in an attractive stucco building at 129 East 64th Street,[16] until his death in 1986. Walk back west on 64th Street to 5th Avenue and turn right.

Automotive genius **John DeLorean** has a magnificent home at 834 5th Avenue.[17] John's connoisseur sports car, named for himself, was produced in Ireland until his company went bankrupt. The building is also home to clothing designer and socialite **Carolyn Roehm** and her husband, mergers-and-acquisitions king **Henry Kravis.** Leave 5th Avenue once again, taking 65th Street a short distance east.

Le Cirque, 58 East 65th Street (212-794-9292), is one of the area's many restaurants that cater to celebrities who enjoy elegant dining in exclusive establishments. Le Cirque is among the top three or four restaurants in the country for stargazing. Movie stars, Presidents, corporate heads, and rock stars make this budget-busting bistro a definite stop on any visit to the Big Apple. Head back west along 65th Street to Madison Avenue and make a right turn.

Le Cirque, 58 E. 65th Street

Need to stop and rest your feet more affordably? Try the Mayfair Coffee Shop at 782 Madison Avenue. Take a seat at the counter and have **Art Carney's** son scramble you up some eggs. **Jerry Lewis** bites into a beefy burger whenever he stops in.

Craving a sweet treat? Try Godiva's gourmet house of chocolates just across the street at 793 Madison Avenue. **Joan Rivers** and her Yorkshire terrier, **Spike,** rarely take a walk without stopping in for a sniff and a lick. **Steven Spielberg** always picks up chocolates for his crew when filming in the area, and **Michael J. Fox** doesn't seem to mind autographing customers' boxes of candy. Walk north to 67th Street, turn left, and head back toward Central Park.

Penthouse publisher **Bob Guccione** lives at 16 East 67th Street[18] in a heavy limestone building that contrasts nicely with the more subtle town houses neaby. Continue to 5th Avenue, turn right, then make another right, and head to 30 East 68th Street,[19] the home of television personality **Mary Stewart.** She resides just off Madison Avenue.

Madison Avenue has some of the most exclusive clothiers

in the world, which is why the rich and famous have little trouble finding their necessities in neighborhood shops. Even if you don't have the $3,000 to shell out for that tailored jacket, you might find it exciting to visit Gianni Versace, 816 Madison Avenue, and look through the styles that gave the "Miami Vice" look to **Don Johnson.** Stars including **Elizabeth Taylor, Billy Joel, Mick Jagger,** and **Phil Collins** stop in from time to time.

Enough shopping, let's get back to stargazing on 5th Avenue. Take 68th Street to 5th Avenue and head north.

Actress **Marlo Thomas** and celebrated talk-show host husband **Phil Donahue,** have moved across Central Park from the star-studded Eldorado at 300 Central Park West to a more sedate building at 875 5th Avenue.[20] Their penthouse residence offers a breathtaking view of Central Park. Phil presently hosts two talk shows emanating from New York: the Emmy Award–winning "Donahue" program and the "Pozner and Donahue Show" (cohosted by Russian journalist Vladimir Pozner). Walk a few doors on 69th Street to our next stop.

··· **I**··
n her late thirties, an independently-minded **Marlo Thomas** met and married talk-show host **Phil Donahue,** whom she fell in love with after appearing on his TV show. Marlo's life has been much like that of her character for four years on the successful sitcom "That Girl": Both were very independent and slow to marry, and both had moved to the Big Apple to pursue an acting career.
··

At 15 East 69th Street,[21] in the Westbury Hotel, resides tennis star **Ilie Nastase.** The late musical-comedy star **Fanny Brice,** subject of the hit Broadway show *Funny Girl,* also had a home here until 1938. Down the block a short distance, at 52 East 69th Street,[22] was the Manhattan residence of bosomy sexpot **Jayne Mansfield.** Continue walking east another block and a half.

To find an actress who best exemplifies New York City, look no further than three-time Tony, onetime Oscar, and onetime Emmy Award–winning actress **Liza Minnelli.** Liza, daughter of legendary star **Judy Garland** and film director **Vincente Minnelli,** who spent her childhood living at the Plaza Hotel and her teenage years (while searching for minor acting roles) at the Barbizon Hotel, presently resides at 150 East 69th Street,[23] *New York, New York* (1977) and *Arthur* (1981) are just two of the movies she's starred in that have been set in Gotham. A former resident of 150 East 69th Street is actress **Doris Lilly,** who resided there until her death in 1991. Sports announcer **Howard Cosell,** best known for the enormous vocabulary he brought to "Monday Night Football" presently resides at that same address. If Howard's language sounds better suited to "Court TV" than to football, don't be surprised—this New York native is a graduate of New York University Law School.

We now head toward 2 East 70th Street,[24] home of two of the world's top clothing designers, **Valentino** and **Oscar de la Renta.** To reach their homes, head back to 5th Avenue, walk north one block to 70th Street, and turn right. **Joan Crawford** spent more than $1 million converting two penthouse condominiums into one while residing here from 1957 until 1959. According to *Mommie Dearest,* the book written by her adopted daughter, **Christina,** Joan had a fetish for cleanliness: Visitors had to take off their shoes at the entrance hall so as not to soil the white rugs, and all flowers and plants were plastic so they could be regularly washed in soapy water. Head one block farther north on 5th Avenue and turn right on 71st Street to arrive at our next stop.

Bill Cosby

Former Miss America **Bess Myerson,** who recently opened a West Side eatery, only to have it close a few months later, resides at 3 East 71st Street.[25] Comedian **Bill Cosby** has his opulent home a few doors east at 18 East 71st Street,[26] where he wakes up most mornings at 4:00 A.M. to jog in Central Park. Bill taped his highly rated television sitcom at the Astoria Studios in Queen, New York. Take Madison Avenue north one block to 72nd Street, turn right, and walk a few blocks to the next location.

East 72nd Street, with its proximity to Central Park and its other amenities, has been a setting for numerous feature films, as well as a home address for many stars. One fourteen East 72nd Street[27] is where **Jon Voight** slipped past the door- man and into **Sylvia Miles's** apartment for a midday rendez- vous in the movie *Midnight Cowboy* (1969). Continue walking east on 72nd Street.

Arlene Dahl, a New York cover girl in the 1940s, later a star of Broadway and the movies, resides at 150 East 72nd Street.[28] Her neighbor, at 160 East 72nd Street,[29] is the actress and former New York radio talk-show host **Joan Fon- taine.** Head south on Lexington Avenue to reach our next stop on the tour.

The Healthy Candle, 972 Lexington Avenue, (212-472- 0970) is a favorite vegetarian takeout spot frequented by health-conscious stars like **Kim Basinger** and her boyfriend, **Alec Baldwin, Demi Moore,** and **Robin Williams.** If you enjoy a flavorful tofu burger and could use a break, seize the moment.

Would you like to get your hair cut while **Woody Allen** or **Howard Cosell** is sitting in the next chair? If so, cross the road to York Barbers, 981 Lexington Avenue, an old-fashioned barbershop where for $17 you can have your hair cut by their favorite stylists. Follow 71st Street east to the next location on the tour.

Audrey Hepburn resided at 171 East 71st Street[30] in the film *Breakfast at Tiffany's* (1961). This simple yet elegant town house remains much the same as it was in the movie. Continue walking east on 71st Street.

New York–born actress **Louise Lasser** appeared in several of ex-husband **Woody Allen's** early films but achieved greatest recognition for starring in the hit soap-opera spoof "Mary Hart- man, Mary Hartman." She has her home at 200 East 71st Street,[31] at the corner of 3rd Avenue. Popular music singer **Lana Cantrell** lives one avenue over, at 300 East 71st Street.[32] We next stroll south down 2nd Avenue to 70th Street, turn right, and head toward 3rd Avenue.

··· **A**···

sked why she chooses to reside in New York as opposed to L.A., **Louise Lasser** mentioned that "Hollywood lacks excitement, it has no neurotic beat all its own, and the leaves don't move. The leaves don't move on the trees. Nothing falls from the sky ever. I like to be in places where things fall from the sky."

··

Singer and actress **Kaye Ballard** lives at 211 East 70th Street, [33] as does television personality **Virginia Graham.** Another resident of this modern highrise is **Sidney Poitier,** the first black matinee idol. Heading west toward Central Park, we come to 162 East 70th Street, the brownstone used as a psychiatrist's office in the 1980 horror film *Dressed to Kill*, which starred **Michael Caine.** We next stroll east back to 3rd Avenue, head south two blocks to 68th Street, and turn eastward.

Pulitzer Prize–winning playwright **Arthur Miller** resides at 215 East 68th Street. [34] This New York native was married to **Marilyn Monroe** for five years, after which he wrote about the agonizing relationship in the play *After the Fall*, which premiered at New York's Repertory Theater in 1964. In the same buliding, four-time Academy Award–winning lyricist **Sammy Cahn** resided until his death in the early part of 1993. The beige walls of Sammy's airy home had been covered with photographs of popular singers who have rendered versions of his many hit tunes. A few doors farther east, at 230 East 68th Street, [35] is the home of "60 Minutes" television reporter **Morley Safer.** Let's now head west, back toward Lexington Avenue, turn left, and take a short walk to our next location.

The Forgotten Woman, 888 Lexington Avenue, is a popular store that supplies overwei—uh, pleasingly plump stars with fabulous fashions to fit their full-fledged figures. **Oprah Winfrey, Roseanne Arnold, Shelley Winters, Julia Child,** and **Beverly Sills** are just a few of the celebrity shoppers. Not long ago, Roseanne and Shelley accidentally met in the store and proceeded to stage an impromptu comic performance that left their fellow customers rolling in the aisles. Head back east on 66th Street to our next stop on the corner of 3rd Avenue.

In a luxury apartment complex called the Manhattan House, 200 East 66th Street, [36] resides comedic actress **Imogene Coca.** This building was also once home to jazz great **Benny Goodman** and to actress **Grace Kelly,** who had previously been residing at the nearby Barbizon Hotel for Women. Continue south on 3rd Avenue one short block.

The Sign of the Dove, 1110 3rd Avenue (212-861-8080), is a gourmet restaurant in a charming building. This wonderfully romantic establishment with its collection of nineteenth-century antiques is popular with celebrities seeking intimacy in a classic setting. Walk west on 65th Street back to Lexington Avenue.

For a less pricey refreshment stop, try Sel & Poivre (212-517-5780) 853 Lexington Avenue. **Beverly Sills, Tony Randall,** and **Jackie Mason** are regulars at this trendy café. (Jackie enjoys making cracks about the French-Jewish chef.) Another choice might be the chichi Mulholland Drive Cafe, 1059 3rd Avenue (212-319-7740), owned by actor **Patrick Swayze,** the haunting hunk who spooked **Demi Moore** in *Ghost* (1990). Retrace your steps east on 65th Street to 3rd Avenue, turn right, and walk a few blocks south if you desire a meal at Patrick's restaurant. From there, we head south to 64th Street and make a left turn.

The florist relied upon by East Side movie stars and socialites is Renny, 159 East 64th Street. **Anne Bass, Diana Ross,** and **Calvin Klein** are a few of the regular customers for the shop's exquisite floral arrangements.

Stroll east to 3rd Avenue, head one block south to 63rd Street, turn left, and walk to 212 East 63rd,[37] the residence of fashion photographer **Francesco Scavullo.** Continue back on 3rd Avenue, heading south to 62nd Street and making a right turn.

The array of superstars and world-renowned writers who live on East 62nd Street can whet any stargazer's appetite. At 165 East 62nd Street[38] resides heartthrob **Brooke Shields,** a native New Yorker who frequents many of the city's trendy clubs and restaurants. She was still in diapers when her career was launched by neighbor Scavullo, who shot her for an Ivory Snow commercial. She soon became the "Ivory Snow Baby" and, by age thirteen, was starring in feature films.

Did **Greta Garbo** *foretell the future when she stopped to pat and admire a beautiful baby in a carriage on 52nd Street? The infant being wheeled was none other than* **Brooke Shields.**

Brooke's neighbor, a few doors east at 200 East 62nd Street,[39] at the corner of 3rd Avenue, is actress **Peggy Cass,** often seen as a guest panelist on game shows.

Plaintiff **Peggy Cass** *was awarded $460,000 in a 1985 lawsuit against a physician at New York's Lenox Hill Hospital. "I'll never play a nun again," the gimpy actress moaned. "I can't kneel." The daydreaming doc had operated on the wrong knee— a goof that left Peggy, who almost became a nun, and then played one in three productions, unable to kneel in her role in* Agnes of God *(1985).*

East 62nd Street is a road for writers. At 201 East 62nd Street[40] is the home of best-selling author **Rona Jaffe.** A few doors east, at 229 East 62nd Street,[41] lives comedian **David Brenner,** who has several books to his name. The most renowned writer on the block is **Tom Wolfe,** founder of the "new journalism" and author of *Bonfire of the Vanities,* the controversial novel that summed up the 1980s. Tom lives at 232 East 62nd Street[42] with his trademark collection of starched shirts and white suits. Walk back to 3rd Avenue, turn left, and take a short stroll south.

Perhaps Tom shops at Bloomingdale's, 1000 3rd Avenue, a great place to spend an afternoon shopping and celebrity-watching. The cosmetics counter, **Estée Lauder's** spa, and the

bloomingdale's

five Bloomies restaurants attract the likes of **Diana Ross, Liza Minnelli, Joan Rivers, Cheryl Tiegs,** and **Jackie Onassis.** A number of movies have been filmed in and around the store, which takes up an entire square block, including *Moscow on* *the Hudson* (1984), starring **Robin Williams,** who played a Russian musician attempting to defect to the West.

We're in the home stretch. Need a snack to get you to the tour's finish line? Relax and enjoy gourmet ice cream at Serendipity 3, 225 East 60th Street (212-838-3531). This combination restaurant-boutique attracts stars including **Larry Hagman, Linda Gray, Barbra Streisand,** and **Cher.** Cher had her party for the movie *Moonstruck* (1987) at this fun eatery and the late **Andy Warhol** used to sketch here while satisfying his sweet tooth. The restaurant is on 60th Street just a half a block east of Bloomingdale's.

serendipity 3

A brisk ten-to-fifteen-minute walk brings us to 425 East 63rd Street, 43 home to actress **Myrna Loy,** voted "Queen of the Movies" in a poll conducted by **Ed Sullivan.** To reach Myrna's residence, walk east on 60th Street to 1st Avenue, turn left, head north three blocks to 63 Street, and turn right. Five blocks south and just east of 1st Avenue, at 425 East 58th Street, 44 is the residence of **Ginger Rogers,** whose ten-movie partnership with **Fred Astaire** has thrilled audiences for decades. Returning three blocks north to 61st Street and heading west from 1st Avenue to 2nd Avenue takes us to the final stop on the tour.

Stiff and sore from your high-class hike? Stop in for a steam, shower, and massage at the Vertical Club. If ever there was a health club packed with major stars, the Vertical Club, 330 East 61st Street, fits that description. Stars like **Bill**

Cosby, Brooke Shields, and **Cher,** and even professional athletes such as **Jimmy Connors** and **Chris Evert,** have all taken advantage of this posh urban country club.

After relaxing at the health club, your best bet to catch a bus downtown is to walk west on 61st Street to 2nd Avenue; for the uptown bus, walk east to 1st Avenue. The closest subway station (N, R, 4, 5, or 6) is reached by heading west on 61st Street to Lexington Avenue and south to 59th Street.

T O U R 7

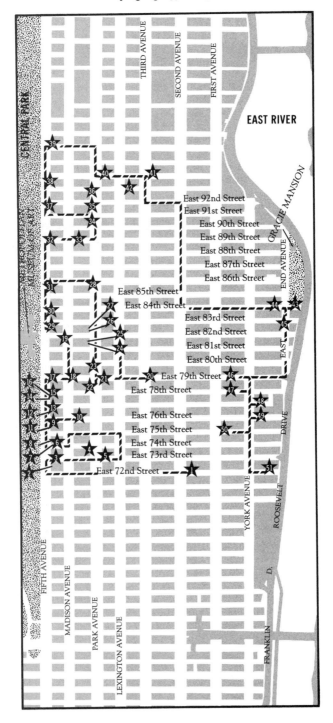

EAST RIVER

CENTRAL PARK

THIRD AVENUE

SECOND AVENUE

FIRST AVENUE

GRACIE MANSION

East 92nd Street
East 91st Street
East 90th Street
East 89th Street
East 88th Street
East 87th Street
East 86th Street

East 85th Street
East 84th Street

East 83rd Street
East 82nd Street
East 81st Street
East 80th Street

East 79th Street
East 78th Street

East 76th Street
East 75th Street
East 74th Street
East 73rd Street
East 72nd Street

END AVENUE

EAST

FIFTH AVENUE

MADISON AVENUE

PARK AVENUE

LEXINGTON AVENUE

YORK AVENUE

ROOSEVELT

FRANKLIN

D.

DRIVE

CLASSIC FILM STARS
UPPER UPPER EAST SIDE

T O P ★10★ T E N
STARS IN THE AREA

Woody Allen ☆ Mel Brooks ☆ Glenn Close ☆ Rodney
Dangerfield ☆ Madeline Kahn ☆ Bill Murray ☆ Paul Newman
☆ Anthony Quinn ☆ Robert Redford ☆ Elizabeth Taylor

NUMBER	ADDRESS	NAME
1	315 East 72nd Street	Elizabeth Taylor
2	920 5th Avenue	Gloria Swanson (deceased)
3	11 East 73rd Street	Roy Scheider
4	778 Park Avenue	William F. Buckley, Jr.
5	118 East 73rd Street	Gloria Steinem
6	23 East 74th Street	Dorothy Parker (deceased) Lena Horne
7	6 East 74th Street	Tammy Grimes
8	930 5th Avenue	Woody Allen
9	944 5th Avenue	Barbara Walters
10	35 East 76th Street	*Hannah and Her Sisters*
11	945 5th Avenue	Gelsey Kirkland Claudette Colbert
12	950 5th Avenue	Anne Bass
13	955 5th Avenue	Robert Redford
14	960 5th Avenue	Claus von Bulow
15	965 5th Avenue	Charles Grodin
16	969 5th Avenue	Glenn Close
17	9 East 79th Street	Art Garfunkel
18	50 East 79th Street	Geraldine Fitzgerald
19	1080 Madison Avenue	Ben Gazzara
20	225 East 79th Street	Gene Shalit
21	109 East 79th Street	Dick Cavett Carrie Nye
22	888 Park Avenue	Caroline Kennedy
23	903 Park Avenue	Ruth Warrick
24	941 Park Avenue	Tom Brokaw
25	955 Park Avenue	Regis Philbin
26	970 Park Avenue	Marvin Hamlisch
27	975 Park Avenue	Madeline Kahn

28	1021 Park Avenue	Paloma Picasso Neil Sedaka
29	1016 5th Avenue	Stella Adler (deceased) Julia Meade
30	1025 5th Avenue	Gavin McLeod
31	1040 5th Avenue	Jackie Onassis
32	17 East 89th Street	Sally Kirkland
33	50 East 89th Street	Mel Brooks Anne Bancroft Tommy Tune
34	1120 Park Avenue	Bill Beutel
35	1155 Park Avenue	Stockard Channing
36	1172 Park Avenue	Ira Levine
37	1107 5th Avenue	Ralph Lauren
38	1120 5th Avenue	Paul Newman Joanne Woodward
39	8 East 96th Street	Bill Murray
40	125 East 94th Street	Erica Jong
41	200 East 94th Street	Eddie Fisher
42	179 East 93rd Street	Marx Brothers (deceased)
43	10 Gracie Square	Gloria Vanderbilt
44	519 East 84th Street	Walter Cronkite
45	60 East End Avenue	Anthony Quinn
46	435 East 79th Street	Joe Cocker
47	420 East 78th Street	James Cagney (deceased)
48	500 East 77th Street	Leslie Gore
49	530 East 76th Street	Rodney Dangerfield
50	407 East 75th Street	Richard Avedon
51	541 East 72nd Street	George Plimpton

Discreet, quiet, and exclusive, the Upper, Upper East Side is a natural home for many screen legends. Where else in New York can one sense the city's throbbing pulse one moment and so easily escape it the next? The final leg of our tour will take us to homes of busy stars who find tranquility in apartments that overlook the East River and Carl Schurz Park.

A focal point of the neighborhood is Museum Mile, a string of magnificent institutions along 5th Avenue between 75th and 92nd streets. Among them are the illustrious Metropolitan, **Frank Lloyd Wright's** extraordinary Guggenheim, and the Cooper-Hewitt Museum. A concentration of superstars have taken up residence all along this strip, which has served as a setting for many feature films.

Our tour begins at 315 East 72nd Street, home to actress

Elizabeth Taylor, and culminates at **George Plimpton's** residence, 541 East 72nd Street. We'll cover an area bounded on the west by 5th Avenue and on the east by the East River. Seventy-second Street is the southern boundary and 96th Street is the northern limit.

Starting Address:	**72nd Street and 2nd Avenue**
Length of Tour:	**3 Hours, 40 Minutes**
Best Starting Time:	**10:00 A.M. or Noon**
Subway:	**6 to 68th Street**
Bus:	**15, 30, 72, 101, or 102**
Bring Along:	**Comfortable shoes, sketch pad, an art-history book, and some of Paul Newman's gourmet popcorn**

☆ THE TOUR

Our journey begins just off the northeast corner of 72nd Street and 2nd Avenue. The best way to reach this location is by using the 72nd Street crosstown bus or the 2nd Avenue bus heading south. If you prefer the subway, the stop (#6 train) at Lexington Avenue and 68th Street is a short walk: Three blocks north on Lexington and two blocks east on 2nd will take you here.

Elizabeth Taylor, whose posh apartment is at 315 East 72nd Street[1] has always had an intimate relationship with Gotham. Whether she's appearing in a Broadway play, such as the 1983 revival of **Noel Coward's** *Private Lives,* in which she starred with two-time spouse *Richard Burton,* or acting in one of her many New York–based films, Liz loves spending time in the Big Ap-

Elizabeth Taylor

ple. Her most important project in the city of late has been to raise funds for the American Foundation for AIDS Research, AMFAR, an organization she helped found.

Elizabeth resides near Gotham's celebrity Chinese restaurant, Fu's, 1395 2nd Avenue (212-517-9670), a few doors north of 72nd Street. Check it out one evening for dinner. Who knows? You might be sitting in the same chair **Paul Newman** occupied the night before. Glance over at table 23— it's **Mel Brooks's** favorite. **Catherine Deneuve, Sidney Poitier,** or **John Kennedy, Jr.,** might also be dining at this elegant Asian eatery.

Now let's head west on 72nd Street toward 5th Avenue, where stargazing is at its best. **Gloria Swanson** made 920 5th Avenue② her principal residence until her death at the ripe old age of eighty-four. The revered actress was always proud to live in New York and displayed that pride through various involvements here: She starred in many Broadway plays, created her own New York–based cosmetics company, and hosted a talk show on a local television station. As we continue north up 5th Avenue, turn onto 73rd Street and head east.

Roy Scheider lives at 11 East 73rd Street③ in an Italian Renaissance mansion built in 1904 for newspaper magnate **Joseph Pulitzer.** Roy began his acting career in New York by appearing on Off-Broadway and Off-Off-Broadway stages. Farther east, we come to Park Avenue.

At 778 Park Avenue④ you find the sumptuous apartment of **William F. Buckley, Jr.,** the noted conservative columnist and host of TV's "Firing Line." Head back down Park Avenue and turn left onto 73rd Street. **Gloria Steinem,** the influential author and feminist, lives with her cat, **Magritte,** at 118 East 73rd Street⑤ in a duplex crammed with books. Walk east on 73rd Street to Lexington Avenue and turn left.

... **S** ....
expert **Ruth Westheimer** *has a huge following but a tiny build. Known as an author and talk-show host, the diminutive doctor is also credited with the creation of the Dr. Ruth Pillow. East Side restaurants, such as Hulots, 1007 Lexington Avenue, are delighted to pile three or four tablecloths on her chair so that the bubbly therapist can more easily reach her champagne.*
....

Care for a $125 sandwich? If so, head for William Poll gourmet caterers at 1051 Lexington Avenue and ask for a beluga caviar on rye to go (hold the mayo, please!). Manhattan socialites and major stars such as **Lauren Bacall, Cheryl Tiegs,** and **Christie Brinkley** consider William Poll a critical resource in planning any successful dinner party.

If caviar isn't your style but you still don't mind spending those few extra dollars for lunch, visit Mortimer's, 1057 Lexington Avenue (212-517-6400). Mortimer's is known around town as a favorite club for "ladies who lunch" and their celebrity friends. Sit at one of the corner tables and eavesdrop—discreetly, please—on the latest society gossip. Take Lexington Avenue north to 75th Street, make a left turn, and head two blocks west to Madison Avenue.

The Whitney Museum of American Art, Madison Avenue at Seventy-fifth Street, stands out from its surroundings because of its stark fortresslike appearance. It showcases an excellent permanent collection of twentieth-century American art, as well as constantly changing special exhibits.

Madison Avenue is known worldwide for its elegant shops, and Givenchy, 954 Madison Avenue, diagonally across from the Whitney Museum, is certainly one of the classiest. When a New York socialite needs that perfect gown to wear to the season's top charity function, a visit to here is mandatory. Perhaps **Hubert de Givenchy** himself will attend to her needs, as the Paris designer flies in frequently to supervise the shop's operation. Continue north on Madison Avenue.

Andy Warhol was a major collector of antiques, so he was a regular visitor at Vito Giallo Antiques at 962 Madison. Other famous clients enjoy viewing the unusual and unique items on display.

Turn back around and head one block down Madison Avenue to 74th Street. Heading west toward 5th Avenue on 74th Street, we find the Volney, a former residence hotel that was home to writer **Dorothy Parker** until her death in 1967. This 23 East 74th Street⑥ address is presently home to **Lena Horne.** The ageless singer, who was born in Brooklyn, began her career at Harlem's fabled Cotton Club and Apollo Theater.

Uptown's hippest Italian restaurant is Coco Pazzo, a high-priced family-style café at 23 East 74th Street (212-794-0205). **Don Johnson, Melanie Griffith, Billy Baldwin,** and a number of music-world greats help make this location primo for those who enjoy celebrity-watching.

Across the street, in an elegant building at 6 East 74th Street, ⑦ resides smoky-voiced actress **Tammy Grimes,** a Tony Award winner. Our next stop is on the northeast corner of 74th Street and 5th Avenue.

If a contest was held to find the person who best exemplifies the creativity, intellectual depth, and individuality that set

New Yorkers apart, **Woody Allen** would far outpace the competitors. This brilliant writer-comedian-actor-director lives simply in an elegant complex at 930 5th Avenue,⑧ just a subway ride from his childhood home in Brooklyn, where he was born Allen Konigsberg.

… **W**……………………………………………………
*hen a young beautiful actress moved to Gotham in search of fame, her fairy godfather turned out to be **Woody Allen.** A reluctant doorman at the director's building took a letter from this inexperienced small-town performer and within twenty-four hours she received an acting job from the man she now calls "Woody the Great." Present-day aspirants be warned, however, that building policy has since changed: Nothing is accepted, no exceptions.*
……………………………………………………

A great place for Woody-watching is Michael's Pub, 211 East 55th Street, where he plays the jazz clarinet every Monday night. He was making music there the night he won two Oscars for the movie *Annie Hall* (1977), and was thus unable to collect his awards personally that evening. Continue north on 5th Avenue.

… **S**……………………………………………………
*ightings of **Woody Allen** in Manhattan are common and sometimes quite humorous. One doorman spotted the reclusive co-median doing cartwheels to entertain a lady as he exited the park.*
……………………………………………………

Barbara Walters, the immensely successful television journalist, has become one of Manhattan's society elite. This fascinating lady lives at 944 5th Avenue⑨ in a very fashionable space with more than enough footage for both Barbara and her attractive daughter, **Jackie.** Barbara chose to send Jackie to Dalton, a neighborhood prep school with a reputation that is tops among New York's upper crust. Stars stay at the Carlyle Hotel, 35 East 76th Street⑩ because they enjoy the attentive yet discreet service. So civilized! To reach

944 Fifth Avenue

The Carlyle

the hotel, turn right onto 76th Street and walk to Madison Avenue. The hotel is also known for the elegant Cafe Carlyle, where singer-pianist **Bobby Short** is usually the featured entertainer. Scenes from *Hannah and Her Sisters* (1986), with **Dianne Wiest** and **Woody Allen,** were shot at the Carlyle. Regular guests include **Marlon Brando, Tom Selleck, George C. Scott,** and **Warren Beatty.** Retrace your steps back to 5th Avenue.

955 Fifth Avenue

Nine forty-five 5th Avenue[11] is home to dancer **Gelsey Kirkland,** as well as to movie great **Claudette Colbert.** Claudette, who came to New York from Paris in 1911, started in the theater, which she still considers her first love. **Anne Bass,** the premiere New York City socialite, resides close by in a very classic home at 950 5th Avenue.[12] Continue walking north.

When **Robert Redford** began his studies at Manhattan's American Academy of Dramatic Arts, he was a student not of acting but of stage design. The handsome young man soon switched to acting, however, and appeared on Broadway in *Barefoot in the Park.* When the **Neil Simon** play was later adapted for the screen (1967), Robert was again cast, this time opposite **Jane Fonda.** Now active as both an actor and an Academy Award–winning director, Robert maintains a home at 955 5th Avenue.[13]

Robert Redford

R..
....**R**..
obert Redford *summed up his feelings toward Gotham when he stated, "I'm like a fish out of water when I'm not here. New York is my water. I need it for survival."*
....

Robert's neighbor, at 960 5th Avenue⑭ is **Claus von Bulow,** the dapper socialite twice tried for attempting to make his wife's social life very quiet indeed. Claus, whose eerie story was retold in the 1990 film *Reversal of Fortune*, lives in a very large residence with extrahigh ceilings for extraswank entertaining.

   Charles Grodin, who lives at 965 5th Avenue,⑮ was a classmate of **Dustin Hoffman's** when he studied acting in New York under **Lee Strasberg.** At 969 5th Avenue⑯ resides **Glenn Close,** whose acting career began with an appearance in the New York theatrical production of *Love for Life*. Coincidentally, this talented performer costarred in *Reversal of Fortune*, in which she played **Sunny von Bulow,** wife of Glenn's neighbor Claus. Our journey next takes us east along 79th Street.

Glenn Close

969 Fifth Avenue

   79th Street is a very popular street among celebrities. **Art Garfunkel,** who was born in Forest Hills, New York, has a home at 9 East 79th Street. ⑰ His building is across 5th Avenue from a heavily used pedestrian and auto entrance to Central Park. The first time he and **Paul Simon** teamed up was in a sixth-grade production of *Alice in Wonderland*. **Geraldine Fitzgerald** chose to live in New York City instead of Hollywood because she despised the commercialism of the L.A. scene. A resident of 50 East 79th Street, ⑱ the veteran actress has become an integral element in the development of New York City street theater. Turn onto Madison Avenue and head north one block.

... **A**rt *Garfunkel* and **Paul Simon** *live directly across from each other, with Central Park in between. In 1983, they had a reunion concert in the park that attracted nearly half a million fans. When Paul returned to the locale for a concert in 1991, he decided to perform without the services of his old partner. A disappointed Art, whose apartment has a perfect aerial view of the concert site, chose to be out of town on that date.*

Need to sit down and grab a snack? Try E.A.T., a restaurant at 1064 Madison Avenue (212-772-0022) that draws a star-studded lunch crowd. If you fancy a delectable yet casual lunch and hunger to hobnob with the likes of **Phil Collins, Bette Midler, Barbra Streisand,** and **David Bowie,** this is the place. Continue walking north.

If you're a celebrity who craves a stylish send-off, the Frank E. Campbell Funeral Home, 1076 Madison, is the only choice. **Judy Garland's** trip over the rainbow was one of the most extravagant productions the home has ever hosted: Over

Frank E. Campbell Funeral Home
1076 Madison Avenue

twenty thousand faithful fans lined up to see the star through her glass-topped casket. Other notables Campbell's has laid to rest include **James Cagney, Joan Crawford, Rudolph Valentino,** and **Montgomery Clift.**

Ben Gazzara once spent years dying—on TV, that is, starring in the weekly drama "Run for Your Life" as a man stricken with a terminal illness. Ben, a star of Broadway as well as Hollywood, grew up on New York's Lower East Side, just a few miles south of his current residence at 1080 Madison Avenue.[19] We now head east on 81st Street two blocks to Lexington Avenue, turn right, and walk two blocks south.

Strakes Flowers, 1140 Lexington Avenue, is a favorite among neighborhood celebrities. **Art Garfunkel** comes specially for anemones, while **Angie Dickinson** varies her selections. **Mariel Hemingway** orders flowers for her nearby restaurant and **Sandy Duncan** always jokes with florists about opening her own shop.

One block east of the flower shop, just past 3rd Avenue, at 225 East 79th Street,[20] is the home of popular film critic **Gene Shalit.** Born in New York City, Gene loves the reaction he receives from fans admiring his walruslike mustache and bouffant Brillo-like hairdo. Turn around and head west on 79th Street.

The next stop is **Dick Cavett's** home at 109 East 79th Street.[21] The cerebral talk-show host resides with his actress wife, **Carrie Nye,** whom he met at Yale University. We now head to Park Avenue, turn left, and walk one block.

Eight eighty-eight Park Avenue[22] is the residence of **Caroline Kennedy,** daughter of the late **President John F. Kennedy.** Her home's location isn't surprising considering the close relationship she has with her mom, **Jackie,** who lives just blocks away. Change directions and head north up Park Avenue to the home of movie actress and soap star **Ruth Warrick,** who resides at 903 Park Avenue.[23] Continue north.

Tom Brokaw,[24] the NBC nightly newscaster, anchors his life at 941 Park Avenue. His wife, **Meredith,** once Miss South Dakota, owns a nearby toy store named the Penny Whistle. Bronx-born **Regis Philbin,** costar of TV's popular "Live with Regis and Kathie Lee," began his career as a page on **Steve Allen's** original "Tonight Show." Regis has a luxurious home at 955 Park Avenue,[25] which he shares with wife, Joy, and two daughters.

· · · **A**· ·

re you talking to me? Are you talking to me?'' shouted **Regis Philbin** *as he awaited movie stardom in a film with newfound buddy Bobby (**Robert DeNiro**) that was being shot at Elaine's Restaurant. After eight anxious hours, Regis was called to fulfill his lifetime dream. On camera, he spoke the now-immortal words* Thank you, *after which he was thanked, given union wages, and told to let go of the chair and go home. The movie being filmed was* Night in the City. *(1992).*

· ·

At 970 Park Avenue ㉖ lives **Marvin Hamlisch,** a New York City native who was the youngest student ever to enroll at the Juilliard School of Music. The award-winning composer is best known for writing the scores of the hit Broadway musical *A Chorus Line,* as well as the scores for the movies *The Sting* (1973) and *The Way We Were* (1973). Also in the building reside actor **Tony Roberts** and Broadway producer **David Merrick.** Our journey north continues.

Stage and screen star **Madeline Kahn** has her home across the street at 975 Park Avenue, ㉗ not far from the home of **Mel Brooks,** who has directed her in many feature films.

Paloma Picasso, the stylish jewelry designer and daughter of the world-renowned Spanish painter **Pablo Picasso,** has her home at 1021 Park Avenue. ㉘ In the same building lives singer-songwriter **Neil Sedaka.** Take 86th Street west to 5th Avenue and head south.

Metropolitan Museum of Art

How about a visit the Metropolitan Museum of Art. It's one of the largest museums in the world and still growing. While the structure's exquisite exterior has served as a backdrop for a number of movies—for example, *The Clock,* a 1945 romance—the Met's interior has always been off limits to any director wishing to film among its priceless paintings.

Across the street from the Metropolitan Museum, at 1016 5th Avenue, ㉙ is the home of television personality **Julia Meade. Stella Adler,** whose acting school has trained some of

America's most famous stars, also resided there up until her death in December 1992.

A few doors up, at 1025 5th Avenue,⃝30 lives actor **Gavin McLeod,** ship's captain in the popular television show "Love Boat." Continue walking north.

Almost every New Yorker has an interesting story about sighting **Jacqueline Kennedy Onassis.** During my interviews, shopkeepers and restaurant owners were only too happy to gloat about the time Jackie O came around. This remarkable and mysterious woman, a resident of 1040 5th Avenue,⃝31 keeps busy working as an editor at Doubleday and volunteering for several New York charities.

We now turn off 5th Avenue and head to 17 East 89th Street,⃝32 home to irrepressible actress **Sally Kirkland.** On the way to Sally's, you pass the striking spiral of the Solomon R. Guggenheim Museum, 1071 Fifth Avenue, between 88th and 89th streets, designed by **Frank Lloyd Wright.** Heading farther down 89th Street, we come to Madison Avenue.

Celebrities are picky when it comes to lingerie, so it's no surprise that Roberta's, 1251 Madison Avenue, is a popular source. **Sally Kirkland** is a regular client. **Kevin Bacon** isn't afraid to help his girlfriend pick out sexy outfits, and **Joanne Woodward** relishes the wide selection of lacy slips the store offers. Continue east on 89th Street.

At 50 East 89th Street,⃝33 you'll find the residence of Brooklyn-born **Mel Brooks,** who began his career playing drums in the Borscht Belt, a group of kosher resorts that once dotted the Catskill Mountains in upstate New York. Producer, writer, director, and actor, this comic one-man band lives with his beautiful wife, actress **Anne Bancroft.** The same 89th Street building is also home to a Broadway choreographer and dancer, the very tall **Tommy Tune.** Walk farther east along 89th Street, crossing Park Avenue.

... **M**..
el Brooks's most embarrassing moment took place in New York's Stage Deli as he was sipping a Cel-Ray soda. A gentleman had shoved a piece of paper at him, so Mel, happy to give an autograph, asked for a pencil and the fellow's name. After the man replied, "Ervoon," Mel wrote on paper, "To Irving, All the best, Mel Brooks." Only later did the flustered comedian realize that the supposed fan, who could hardly speak English, was only seeking directions.

....

New York celebrities for the most part send their children to private schools. Perhaps the favorite such academy is the Dalton School, 108 East 89th Street, one of whose most generous supporters was the late conductor **Leonard Bernstein.** If you pass by in the early morning or late afternoon, check out the parade of limousines. Head back to Park Avenue and proceed north one block.

Eleven twenty Park Avenue ㉞ is a stately building that is the home of newscaster **Bill Beutel.** If you're a fan of **Stockard Channing,** take a short stroll north over to 1155 Park Avenue ㉟ and see the residence of this New York–born actress. If you would enjoy knowing where author **Ira Levine** (*Rosemary's Baby*) has his digs, head a few hundred yards up to 1172 Park Avenue. ㊱ Otherwise, start your feet in the direction of Central Park. Head west via 91st Street.

On your way westward, you might hanker for a prairie-sized burger. If so, stop at Jackson Hole, 1270 Madison Avenue, (212-427-2820) at the southwest corner of 91st Street, for a reasonably priced meal. **Woody Allen** filmed a humorous lunch scene there for the movie *Hannah and Her Sisters* (1986), and **Sidney Sheldon** has a character in one of his novels mention this popular grill. Actor **Christian Slater** creates havoc whenever he stops in: Female customers go crazy, and waitresses are too busy gawking to get any work done. Whenever MTV's **"Downtown" Julie Brown** visits, she's very friendly and happy to talk to everyone. **Paul Newman** and **Joanne Woodward** enjoy the restaurant's food but rarely eat there—they prefer to have the burgers delivered to their nearby apartment. Continue along 91st Street.

Paul Newman

The Carnegie mansion at 2 East 91st Street, built in 1898 as a sixty-four room home for Andrew Carnegie, now houses the Cooper-Hewitt Museum. This magnificent structure appeared as the Russian embassy in the movie *Marathon Man* (1976), which starred **Dustin Hoffman.** We finally arrive at 5th Avenue. Head north.

Fashion designer **Ralph Lauren** lives at 1107 5th Avenue, (37) a number of blocks north of the boutique that bears his name. This building originally boasted a fifty-four-room penthouse apartment with a private elevator to a ground-level driveway. The extravagant arrangement was designed to serve the building's first owner, **Mrs. E. F. Hutton.**

Superstar actor, salad-dressing king, and racecar driver **Paul Newman** has his home at 1120 5th Avenue.(38) He began his illustrious career in New York City doing minor roles in television. Before making his mark in movies like *Cat on a Hot Tin Roof* (1958), *Hud* (1963), and *Cool Hand Luke* (1967), Paul was a Broadway understudy in the play *Picnic.* Another *Picnic* stand-in was **Joanne Woodward,** and the pair soon fell in love and married. Joanne, known for her tireless work on behalf of charitable causes, contributes much of the financing for Dancers, a New York ballet company. This pair of down-to-earth stars is spotted often at restaurants and shops all over the East Side. Turn right onto 94th Street.

Songwriter **George S. Kaufman** occupied at home at 14 East 94th Street during the late 1920s. Return to 5th Avenue, head north two blocks, and turn right onto 96th Street. At 8 East 96th Street(39) is the residence of comic actor **Bill Murray.** Bill's first break came in 1975 when he was hired to make people laugh on the National Lampoon radio show, but his career really took off when he became a regular on "Saturday Night Live."

Bill Murray

***Bill Murray** ordered some supplies from the 90th Street Pharmacy on Madison Avenue. When the delivery boy came, Bill discovered he had little money for a tip, so he rewarded the lad with a loaf of white bread.*

Let's now take a short walk east over to Park Avenue; then go two blocks south and a few doors left, arriving at 125 East 94th Street,④⓪ residence of **Erica Jong,** author of the controversial book *Fear of Flying.* **Eddie Fisher,** as well known for the women he's married and divorced (Elizabeth Taylor, Debbie Reynolds) as he is for his singing voice, has his home at 200 East 94th Street,④① at the corner of 3rd Avenue. Head one block south on 3rd Avenue to 93rd Street, turn right, and walk a few doors west to our next stop.

E *ddie Fisher has an outstanding IOU for a bowl of soup at a nearby bagel shop. "Put it on my tab," he ordered the cashier on a day long ago. When I was told the two dollars had never been paid, I asked the management to place it on my own tab, along with a few other items, under the name Kris Kringle.*

The **Marx Brothers** spent their childhood at 179 East 93rd Street.④② They left the Big Apple in 1910, when their mother, Minnie, decided to move the family's vaudeville act to Chicago. Turn your feet around and return east to 3rd Avenue, make a right turn, and head to 92nd Street.

It's time for a well-deserved break. How about Third Avenue Bagel, 3rd Avenue and 92nd Street, (212-534-0200) for some authentic New York cuisine? Regulars here include **Rick Moranis** (Thursdays), hockey star **Rod Gilbert** (mornings), plus **Gene Hackman, Elizabeth McGovern,** and **Brooke Shields.** Brooke impressed the owner when she made a special visit to the shop with signed photos she'd promised to customers on an earlier trip. We next walk east on 92nd Street to 2nd Avenue and head south three blocks.

T *wenty-year-old Christina Applegate, the flirtatious daughter on television sitcom "Married with Children," was astounded to learn that the Third Avenue Bagel staff had not see her nude layout as Miss April in the 1992 Penthouse Calendar. The starlet quickly purchased a copy from a nearby newstand and brought it back for the young lads to inspect.*

Elaine's, 1703 Second Avenue, (212-534-8103) is the ultimate New York stargazer's restaurant. If you're in the mood for

Italian food amidst Gotham's glitterati, this is the place. The regulars include **Diane Keaton, Chevy Chase, Diana Ross, Shirley MacLaine, Warren Beatty, Mike Nichols, Farrah Fawcett, Kurt Vonnegut, Jacqueline Onassis,** and **Woody Allen.** Mastermind of the restaurant's success is owner **Elaine Kaufman,** who acts as surrogate Jewish mother to many of her famous patrons. Two of the movies filmed in this celebrity hangout include *Network* (1976), starring **Faye Dunaway** and **William Holden,** and *Manhattan* (1979), directed by **Woody Allen.** One

Elaine's, 1703 Second Avenue

recent evening, the entire restaurant was taken over for the filming of *Night in the City* (1992), starring **Robert De Niro.**

The final portion of this tour begins near the East River, fifteen minutes away on foot, five minutes and three dollars by taxi. If walking, head south on 2nd Avenue to 84th Street, turn left, and stroll three block east, crossing East End Avenue.

We begin at 10 Gracie Square,[43] off 84th Street and east of East End Avenue. In that quiet, isolated location resides designer and socialite **Gloria Vanderbilt.** The area's focal point is Gracie Mansion, since 1942 the official residence of New York's mayor, which is located in Carl Schurz Park, along the bank of the East River.

Not far away lives the journalist once considered "the most trusted man in America," former news anchor **Walter Cronkite.** Does Walter say "And that's the way it is" every evening as he kisses his wife, **Betsy** good night in their home at 519 East 84th Street?[44] To reach his residence, return west on 84th Street just past East End Avenue. Next, head back to East End Avenue, turn right, and walk south. At 60 East End Avenue[45] resides a versatile actor best known for his title role in *Zorba the Greek* (1964), **Anthony Quinn.** Continue walking down East End Avenue to 79th Street, turn right, and head west one and a half blocks, crossing York Avenue.

Rock-and-roll singer **Joe Cocker** has a home at 435 East 79th Street.[46] Head back to York Avenue, walk south one block to 78th Street, and continue west. At 420 East 78th Street[47] is a four-story building **James Cagney** lived in when he was a young stage actor. Return to York Avenue and head one block south. At 500 East 77th Street,[48] at the corner of York Avenue, we have the residence of **Leslie Gore.** Continue south on York Avenue to 76th Street, turn left, and head east ot our next stop.

··· **L**eslie Gore *grew up in Tenafly, New Jersey, attending an exclusive private school, enjoying a posh summer camp, and playing with Buffee, her white poodle. At age seventeen, she decided she wanted to be a star, so she handed her wealthy father a tape of "It's My Party," which she sang at her own sweet-sixteen affair. The supportive dad passed the tune on to his old friend Irving Green, head of Mercury Records, who promptly signed the talented youngster to a contract.*

Rodney Dangerfield resides in a modern high rise at 530 East 76th Street.[49] Although this Long Island–born comedian still claims to "get no respect," he does own Dangerfield's, the Manhattan comedy club. Nearby, at 407 East 75th Street,[50] lives **Richard Avedon,** the world-renowned photographer. To reach his home, head south on York Avenue and walk one block west on 75th Street toward 1st Avenue. Journalist **George Plimpton,** whose trademark is to participate in the activity he's chronicling, resides at 541 East 72nd Street.[51] The best route to George's home is to take York Avenue south to 72nd Street and head east.

Our tour ends in a very residential area of New York. Bus service heading crosstown on 72nd Street, as well as north and south on York Avenue, is close at hand. Since the subway is five blocks west on 72nd Street, then three blocks south on Lexington Avenue, it might be the perfect time to splurge on a taxi.

James Cagney

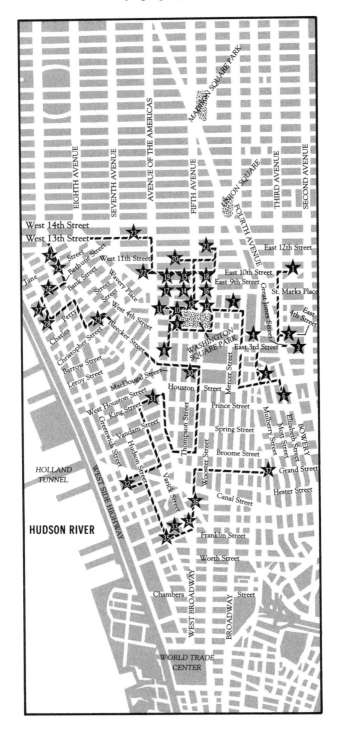

THE CUTTING EDGE

DOWNTOWN

T O P **10** T E N

STARS IN THE AREA

Cher ☆ Harry Connick, Jr. ☆ Tom Cruise ☆ Robert De Niro
☆ Matt Dillon ☆ Richard Gere ☆ Grace Jones ☆ Rob Lowe
☆ Bette Midler ☆ Susan Sarandon

NUMBER	ADDRESS	NAME
1	122 East 10th Street	Karen Allen
2	355 Bowery	Barry Bostwick
3	46 East 3rd Street	Quentin Crisp
4	14 East 4th Street	Cher
		Rob Lowe
		Cheryl Lowe
		Keith Richards
		Jonathan Elias
		Tom Cruise
		Nicole Kidman
5	298 Mulberry Street	Harry Connick, Jr.
6	230 Elizabeth Street	Eric Bogosian
7	300 Mercer Street	Sean Young
8	119 MacDougal Street	*The Godfather, Part II*
		Serpico
9	Washington Square Park	*Barefoot in the Park*
		When Harry Met Sally
10	27 Washington Square North	Matthew Broderick
		Uta Hagen
11	124 Waverly Place	Lauren Hutton
12	One 5th Avenue	Wendy Wasserstein
13	Two 5th Avenue	Ed Koch
14	20 5th Avenue	John Heffernan
15	25 5th Avenue	Brian De Palma
16	25 East 9th Street	Susan Sarandon
		Tim Robbins
17	49 West 9th Street	Matt Dillon
		Victor Ramos
18	26 East 10th Street	Richard Gere
		Cindy Crawford
19	38 West 10th Street	Kathleen Turner
		Jay Weiss
20	35 West 11th Street	Jane Curtin

21	35 East 12th Street	Mikhail Baryshnikov
22	4 Patchin Place	e. e. cummings (deceased)
23	134 West 13th Street	Joe Jackson
24	61 Jane Street	Judd Hirsch
25	317 West 12th Street	Andrew McCarthy
26	27 Bethune Street	Jennifer Grey
27	166 Bank Street	Grace Jones
28	377 West 11th Street	Gregory Hines
29	218 West 10th Street	Terrence McNally
30	184 Thompson Street	Vincent Spano
31	41 King Street	Ally Sheedy Amanda Plummer
32	451 Washington Street	Bette Midler
33	20 North Moore Street	David Letterman
34	14 North Moore Street	*Ghostbusters*
35	110 Hudson Street	Robert De Niro Harvey Keitel Lorraine Bracco
36	260 West Broadway	Cyndi Lauper Isabella Rossellini John F. Kennedy, Jr.
37	240 Centre Street	Cindy Crawford Steffi Graf Winona Ryder

"Girls Just Wanna Have Fun," as sung by Tribeca's very own **Cyndi Lauper,** characterizes the trendy stars who have settled in New York City's exciting downtown. Here is the place tomorrow's stars come to train and today's slip off their public personae and dress up like average human beings.

East Greenwich Village, with its mix of creative young artists and both social and political radicals, is certainly an intriguing place to start our journey. New York University's illustrious Film School has been the training ground for many of America's best filmmakers. **Martin Scorsese, Spike Lee, Chris Columbus,** and **Oliver Stone** learned the art of filmmaking with a purpose in this renowned institution spoofed in the 1990 film *The Freshman.* Crossing to the West Village, the Bohemian spirit is still very much alive but blended in such a way with conventional standards as to make the mix popular to the masses. Farther south, Tribeca is being trailblazed by **Robert De Niro** and other superstars who hunger for an unpretentious and quiet escape from the busy streets north of Canal.

The area to be covered on this tour is bounded by 14th Street on the north, Chambers Street on the south, 1st Avenue on the east, and the Hudson River on the west.

Starting Address:	**10th Street and 2nd Avenue**
Length of Tour:	**4 Hours, 30 Minutes**
Best Starting Time:	**10:00 A.M. or Noon**
Subway:	**L, N, R, 4, or 5 to Union Square**
Bus:	**9, 13, 14, 15, 101 or 102**
Bring Along:	**Beads, change for carrot juice— and be sure to dress casually**

☆ THE TOUR

To reach the first stop on our tour, when coming from Union Square, take 14th Street east three blocks to 2nd Avenue, make a right, then another right onto 10th Street. If you care to relax prior to your journey, there's Union Square Park with its many park benches within a few yards of the subway station. Care for an apple? On Mondays, Wednesdays, and Saturdays, farmers sell their produce at inexpensive prices on the north end of the park.

Talented actress **Karen Allen** lives in a well-kept walk-up building at 122 East 10th Street,① only a few doors over from Cooper Union, a college dedicated to the fields of science and art. Karen and the school are located in the East Village, an area whose cheap rents and iconoclastic ways have for years attracted large numbers of artists, writers, actors, and rock musicians, as well as other people who prefer a life outside the mainstream.

Next take 10th street to 3rd Avenue, and make a left. Head south, past the college on your right-hand side, for seven short blocks. This is where 3rd avenue changes its name to the Bowery, and at 355 Bowery② is the residence of **Barry Bost-wick.** From the exterior of the building, it's hard to imagine the spacious home with its exposed brick walls that this fine actor occupies.

Around the corner and halfway down the block, at 46 East 3rd Street, ③ in a pink four-story walk-up called the Eastwick, lives writer **Quentin Crisp.** If you're allergic to dust, be careful around Quentin's home: He once went "four years without ever cleaning it," or so claimed this author of the 1985 book *Manners from Heaven: A Divine Guide to Good Behavior.*

. . . **Q**uentin Crisp *is serious when citing his reasons for moving to New York from his native England: "Everyone is your friend. When you sit on a bus people ask where are you going. Within moments the entire bus is interested in your destination. What a warm environment!"*

Cher

Take 3rd Street west across the Bowery, past Engine Company 33 on your right, make a right onto Lafayette Street, and one block up, at the southwest corner of 4th Street, is the Silk Building.

It's appropriate for **Cher** to reside in the magnificently restored Silk Building, 14 East 4th Street:④ An easy ride on the elevator down to the first floor and she arrives at Tower Records, which carries a library of the superstar's greatest hits.

A number of scenes from her Academy Award–winning film *Moonstruck* (1987) were staged in the area around her home.

. . . **I** *really enjoy being able to look like hell,"* **Cher** *said as her reason for loving Gotham. "In Beverly Hills, if you dress down, people ask if you've had some sort of medical problem, but in New York, anything goes."*

The Silk Building is also home to clean-cut, charming actor **Rob Lowe** and his new wife, **Cheryl,** a makeup artist. In 1992, Rob enjoyed the luxury of working close to home when he appeared as as a naïve student seduced by a maid in Broadway's *A Little Hotel on the Side.* This nineteenth-century building is home as well to a 1988 Rock and Roll Hall of Fame inductee,

Rob Lowe

The Silk Building, 14 E. 4th Street

Tom Cruise

Rolling Stones guitarist **Keith Richards.** His musical neighbor in the complex is composer **Jonathan Elias.**

Talented actor and touted sex symbol **Tom Cruise** is yet another celebrity listed on the megastar roster of the Silk Building. Tom lives with his wife, beautiful actress **Nicole Kidman.**

A *New York shoe seller thought he'd found a customer to follow in the footsteps of a famed Filipino footwear fetishist. The merchant's hopes for his very own Imelda Marcos were dashed, however, when, of the vast array of shoes he delivered to the home of* **Tom Cruise** *and* **Nicole Kidman,** *all but one pair were returned to the shop.*

Walk south on Lafayette Street about four short blocks to where Mulberry intersects; singer-pianist **Harry Connick, Jr.,** resides a block farther south. This charismatic crooner and his cat live in a modern redbrick building at 298 Mulberry Street⑤ (corner of Houston). Harry's distinctive song stylings

Harry Connick, Jr.

have led critics to see the young performer as heir to the legacy of Ol' Blue Eyes himself, Frank Sinatra.

Walk two blocks east on Houston Street, then make a right onto Elizabeth Street. Two blocks south, in the area of Little Italy, is the home of stage and film actor **Eric Bogosian,** at 230 Elizabeth Street.[6] Not far away, in the heart of the campus of New York University, lives **Sean Young.** To reach her building, head back to Houston Street, west for three blocks to Broadway, make a right, and head four blocks to Waverly Place. A block left will place you there. This frank, sometimes rebellious, young actress, whose high-rise building at 300 Mercer Street[7] closely resembles the student dormitories around it, must feel well suited to life in the center of an institution known for its freethinking spirit.

Our next stop is reached by following Waverly Place to Washington Square Park. On the far south side of the park is MacDougal Street, which we take south a block. You may recognize dingy, dark, and smoky Caffe Reggio, 119

MacDougal Street[8] (212-475-9557) from scenes in *The Godfather, Part II* (1974) and *Serpico* (1973). If you'd like to sip espresso in the first café to be built in America (1785), check

Cafe Reggio, 119 MacDougal Street

out this lively coffeehouse and relax to the sound of classical music. Now head back up to the park.

Newlyweds **Jane Fonda** and **Robert Redford** met in Washington Square Park[9] in the film *Barefoot in the Park* (1967).

This vibrant space was also featured in the 1989 comedy *When Harry Met Sally.* If you visit the park on a sunny day, join the crowds watching the jugglers, mimes, musicians, and comedians who set up shop there and then pass the hat. Maybe another member of the audience will be actor **Matthew Broderick,** who resides across the street on the north side of the park at 27 Washington Square North.[10] Tony Award–winning Matthew, a New York native, caught the acting bug

Arch (erected in 1889)
Washington Square Park

from his well-known father, the late **James Broderick.** In the same complex lives accomplished actress and acting teacher **Uta Hagen.**

On the next block west, over a shoe-repair shop in a brown plastered building at 124 Waverly Place[11] lives supermodel and film star **Lauren Hutton.** When this striking blonde first arrived in New York, she acquired a fuzzy tail in her job as a Playboy Bunny.

Head back two blocks east on Waverly Place to the north side of Washington Square Park and the arch, erected in 1889 for the centennial of George Washington's inauguration as President. A left will bring you to One 5th Avenue,[12] the residence of Pulitzer Prize–winning playwright **Wendy Wasserstein,** author of *The Heidi Chronicles.* Her neighbor, in a gray brick building at Two 5th Avenue,[13] is **Ed Koch,** Gotham's controversial ex-mayor. Never at a loss for words, this opinionated character is well suited to his present roles as newspaper columnist and radio talk-show host.

Continue north to a prewar brick building at 20 5th Avenue,[14] where New York–born stage and film actor **John Heffernan** resides. Nothing mysterious about 25 5th Avenue,[15] even though it's home to **Brian De Palma,** noted director of movie suspense. When Brian directed *Bonfire of the Vanities* (1990), he chose a similar building, also on 5th Avenue but a few miles north, to serve as home to the wealthy socialite played by **Tom Hanks.**

East on 9th Street and a half-block walk brings you to the home of New York–born actress **Susan Sarandon,** who makes her home in a building with a beautiful ornate facade at 25 East 9th Street.⁽¹⁶⁾ After breaking into acting on several soap operas, this naturally talented star has become one of the great actresses in film today. Susan's cohabitant in her cozy quarters is her costar in the 1988 film *Bull Durham,* and coproducer of their 1989 baby boy—**Tim Robbins.** Tim was born and raised in the very same area of Greenwich Village.

... **C**elebrities *tend to use taxis instead of limousines because there's less chance of being spotted": This was* **Tim Robbins's** *answer to a cabdriver's question. Tim and* **Susan Sarandon** *then shifted out of the nosy cabbie's view as they cuddled in the backseat.*

Marylou's

Susan and Tim need only cross 5th Avenue and then walk a few doors west and a few steps down to reach the charming brownstone housing Marylou's, 21 West 9th Street (212-533-0012). The talented couple might well run into some of this sedate restaurant's other regulars, such as **Faye Dunaway, Kathleen Turner,** and **Robert De Niro.** Robert spent many a night listening to jazz and sipping coffee here while filming *Night in the City* (1992) only a few blocks away.

Matt Dillon

Matt Dillon is written about by columnists as much for his acting as he is for owning a midtown nightclub called The Whiskey. This new celebrity hangout is only a few miles from

Matt's home in an elegant five-story townhouse at 49 West 9th Street.[17] Brass and wood adorn the front entrance of this building that for many years served as a women's dormitory. The actor's movie magnetism was discovered by casting director **Victor Ramos,** who found a teenaged Matt while interviewing potential actors in the young hunk's high school. The talent scout eventually signed on to become Matt's personal manager and can these days oversee the star's affairs closely, because both live in the same 9th Street building.

49 W. 9th Street

Head east back to 5th Avenue, make a left, then a right on 10th Street, and at 26 East 10th Street[18] is the home of

Richard Gere

dashingly handsome leading man **Richard Gere.** A home in New York is no accident for Richard, for his first love was the Broadway stage, a goal he dropped out of college to pursue. Richard's "Pretty Woman" (she's got the beauty marks to prove it) is his wife, supermodel **Cindy Crawford.** We now walk west on 10th Street, crossing 5th Avenue.

In a lovely brown town house at 38 West 10th Street[19] lives seductive actress **Kathleen Turner,** known for the wide range of roles she's undertaken in films like *Body Heat* (1981) and *Peggy Sue Got Married* (1986). She resides with her husband, Jay Weiss, a successful realtor and part-time musician. Easygoing Jay is nothing like the the husband Kathleen terrorized so convincingly in the 1989 black comedy *The War of the Roses.* Back to 5th Avenue, north one block, and around the corner takes you to the next stop.

Kathleen Turner

It's the home of television comedienne **Jane Curtin,** who lives in a brick town house painted yellow, with white window trim and a bright red front door. "Saturday Night Live" led to "Kate and Allie" and a career that continues steadily upward. Her colorful dwelling is located at 35 West 11th Street.[20]

Walk east on 11th Street to University Place, make a left, and head one block north. Ready to rest and enjoy a cup of fresh coffee? University Place Restaurant, 101 University Place, (212-475-7727) serves up wholesome grub at inexpensive prices. Grab a table near the window so you don't miss the opportunity to spot one of your favorite entertainers out for a morning or afternoon stroll.

Only a few doors over is the home of **Mikhail Baryshnikov,** who has his residence in a loft-type building with huge windows and heavy black iron gates shielding the front entrance, at 35 East 12th Street.[21] Misha, as he's known to colleagues, is not only one of the greatest ballet dancers ever but has proven capable as an actor, too. He appeared in the hit movie *The Turning Point* (1977) and costarred with **Gregory Hines** in *White Nights* (1985). Our journey now takes us south on University Place to Tenth Street. Turn right there and walk two blocks, crossing Avenue of the Americas.

Between 6th and Greenwich avenues, off West 10th Street, in a picturesque alley filled with charming town houses, is the

4 Patchin Place

former home of one of our century's great poets, **e. e. cummings. Ezra Pound, T. S. Eliot,** and **Dylan Thomas** were among the many other poets to visit this literary genius at 4 Patchin Place,[22] where he lived until his death in 1962.

Our next stop is the home of singer and musician **Joe Jackson,** 134 West 13th Street.[23] Back to the Avenue of the Americas, three blocks north, and a left turn onto 13th Street will take us there. This ultimate music man can sing and play almost any instrument, including piano, saxophone, and guitar.

A cab is not necessary for traveling the few blocks to the doorman building at 61 Jane Street.[24] Just head west on 13th Street to Hudson Street and continue south to the corner of Jane Street. This structure is home to the actor whose starring role helped make TV sitcom "Taxi" a five-year phenomenon— the Emmy and Tony Award–winning **Judd Hirsch.**

In an area of Greenwich Village loaded with avant-garde writers, actors, and musicians lives one of the most successful young actors in film today, **Andrew McCarthy.** Andrew, who lives above a restaurant at 317 West 12th Street,[25] specializes in portraying wealthy students. His residence is one block south, down Hudson Street. Continue south on Hudson Street one block, then around the corner to reach our next stop.

While her famous dad, **Joel,** resides uptown, **Jennifer Grey** prefers the Bohemian atmosphere of Greenwich Village. This naturally talented actress, who captivated audiences with her sensuality in *Dirty Dancing* (1987), has a home at 27 Bethune Street.[26] Her neighbor, at 166 Bank Street,[27] which is one block farther down Washington Street and one block west, is the statuesque, exotically beautiful **Grace Jones.** After an early start as a model on the European circuit, this six-foot-tall native New Yorker developed a huge following among Gotham's hip set through her wild singing performances.

Grace Jones

· · · **A**· ·
n exasperated **Grace Jones** *couldn't persuade anyone at the party that she was, in fact, Grace Jones. Her look-alike brother, Cris, had already arrived—dressed convincingly to resemble his flamboyant sister.*

· ·

From **Grace Jones's,** head south one block to 11th Street, and make a right. New York–born hoofer **Gregory Hines** has his home in a modern brick complex with an awesome view of

the Hudson River at 377 West 11th Street.[28] Gregory's dancing ability, combined with his flair for acting, makes for a very
versatile showman. Now walk east on 11th Street three blocks
to the corner of Hudson Street.

Established Since 1880

Michael J. Fox is one of the many celebrities who enjoy
reliving the tradition of hanging out in the White Horse Tavern, 567 Hudson Street (212-243-9260). Literary lions **Norman Mailer, e. e. cummings, Thomas Wolfe,** and **Dylan
Thomas** anointed this historic bar as their gathering place.
Dylan Thomas is said to have downed eighteen double whis-
keys in the tavern on the very day he died of alcohol poisoning.

A healthier writer, playwright **Terrance McNally,** resides
a few blocks south, at 218 West 10th Street,[29] in a tan brick
building with a firescape out front. His home is easily reached
by heading three blocks south on Hudson Street and then east
on Tenth Street toward Bleecker Street.

A twenty-minute walk south on Bleecker Street or a four-
dollar cab ride will bring you to the home of movie actor
Vincent Spano at 184 Thompson Street.[30] His complex is on
the corner of Thompson and Bleecker streets, in one of the
most hectic areas of the Village.

Walk one block east on Bleecker Street to West Broadway
and turn right. Head south, crossing West Houston, four
blocks to Broome Street. In this area full of trendy art galleries,
known as SoHo (short for South of Houston), is the Cupping
Room Cafe, 359 West Broadway, (212-925-2898) a hidden
gem for stargazers. **Liza Minnelli, Cindy Crawford,** and **Richard Gere, Madonna,** and **Robert DeNiro** enjoy the homey
surroundings and the casual atmosphere of this warm and comfortable restaurant. **John Kennedy, Jr., Willem Dafoe,** and
Matthew Broderick visit this reasonably priced eatery almost
daily. The best time to stop in is weekdays, when there are
no lines.

West on Broome Street to the Avenue of the Americas,
north three blocks, and half a block west on King Street brings
you to the next stop. Actress **Ally Sheedy** resides at 41 King
Street[31] in an attractively remodeled town house. Ally was
born in New York, as was actress and building mate **Amanda
Plummer,** who grew up on nearby Bank Street. Tony Award–

winning Amanda carries on a great Broadway tradition inherited from famous father, **Christopher Plummer** and her mother **Tammy Grimes.**

Bette Midler

Continue west on King Street to Varick Street, turn left, stroll five blocks to Watts Street, and turn right. Three blocks past Canal Street, you come to Washington Street. Actress, singer, and personality **Bette Midler** has her home in a classically elegant building, erected in 1891, at 451 Washington Street.[32] This amazing extrovert is an avid reader who has filled her spacious residence with an array of literary master-

451 Washington Street

pieces. Bette worked as a go-go dancer and a typist before her mentor, **Joe Franklin,** helped her get a job in the chorus of Broadway's *Fiddler on the Roof.* The next stop was New York's Continental Baths, where the Divine Miss M's campy singing was a smash hit with the crowd of gay men in towels.

Witty talk-show host **David Letterman** has his Manhattan residence in a simple building at 20 North Moore Street.[33] His home is in Tribeca, the very trendy area where casualness is the rule. From **Bette Midler's** his home is reached by heading east one block to Greenwich Street. There, turn right, walk south six blocks to North Moore Street, turn left, and proceed a block east, just past Hudson Street.

Down the block from Dave is Hook and Ladder Firehouse 8, located at 14 North Moore Street.[34] You might recall the roof being blown off this building in the film *Ghostbusters* (1984).

The quiet streets of Tribeca are also home to **Robert De Niro,** one of the most brilliant actors ever to hit the silver screen. This powerful two-time Academy Award–winning performer resides within blocks of his childhood home on Manhattan's Lower East Side. He presently lives in the classic stone-columned building at 110 Hudson Street.[35] It's easily reached by walking west one block on North Moore Street, then turning left at Hudson Street, and heading south one block to the corner of Franklin Street.

110 Hudson Street

To bring realism to a role, **Robert De Niro** *will gain fifty pounds or shave his head. In the 1991 film* Cape Fear, *he covered his body with tattoos. The pain suffered by Robert when the tattoos were applied was minimal, however, since artists at TEMPTU, 157 Hudson Street, used brushes, not needles, and only the best of paints.*

Robert De Niro

One ten Hudson Street is also home to Robert's longtime pal **Harvey Keitel.** Both actors were fortunate to study acting for the theater under teaching legend **Stella Adler.** They also appeared together in two films by Martin Scorsese: *Mean Streets* (1973) and *Taxi Driver* (1976). Harvey, although separated from his attractive wife, actress **Lorraine Bracco,** still shares the same residence. Lorraine now has also worked with De Niro in a Scorsese picture: She played **Ray Liotta's** wife in the 1990 gangster epic *Good Fellas.* We next walk one block west on Franklin Street to the corner of Greenwich Street.

Actor **Robert De Niro** plays the role of entrepreneur at 375 Greenwich Street. There, in a multistory warehouse, he opened the trendy celebrity hangout Tribeca Grill (212-941-3900) with coowners **Bill Murray, Sean Penn, Christopher Walken,** and **Mikhail Baryshnikov.** Even though this large brick burger stand is usually packed with stars, the rule of the house is that all customers are treated equally. The same structure also features the Tribeca Film Center, which houses offices and studios devoted to film production. **Steven Spielberg, Ron Howard,** and **Quincy Jones** all have facilities in De Niro's visionary complex.

Heading back east on Franklin Street two blocks to West Broadway, turning left, and walking one block north en route to our next destination, we pass LeRoy's, 247 West Broadway,

(212-966-3370) a clean, inexpensive diner where you might want to use the rest room, make a phone call, or have a quick bite. Area residents including **Cyndi Lauper** and **Robert De Niro** like to stop in for the eggs. One recent morning, **John Kennedy, Jr.,** didn't seem to mind signing autographs for two excited young ladies before attacking his eggs-over-easy.

After breakfast, **Cyndi Lauper** crosses the street to her home in the luxurious American Thread Building, 260 West

American Thread Building, 260 West Broadway

Broadway.③⑥ The high ceilings and solid block walls of this 1896 edifice, once headquarters to the Wool Exchange, are perfect for this madcap songstress to unloose her vocal cords. Cyndi, grew up in Queens, walked horses at New York's Belmont Racetrack, and cleaned dog kennels before hitting it big in show business. Also in the building resides the radiant and sensous actress and model, **Isabella Rossellini,** daughter of film star **Ingrid Bergman** and director **Roberto Rossellini.** Dashing public prosecutor John F. Kennedy, Jr., son of the late president and chosen by *People* as the handsomest man in America, is the building's newest celebrity. Next, head one and a half blocks north to Grand Street, and seven blocks east to Centre Street.

Cyndi Lauper

The Police Building, 240 Centre Street,③⑦ (built in 1909) once the main headquarters for the New York City Police Department has been converted (1988) into residences for the rich and famous. The grand complex is topped off with an imposing dome. Young talented actress **Winona Ryder** (born Winona Laura Horowitz) has a spacious home in the police building. Blonde-haired blue-eyed tennis star **Steffi Graf** also resides in the complex. Model **Cindy Crawford** never relinquished her residence in the building even though she maintains another home with husband **Richard Gere.**

There's plenty of public transit in the area to whisk you away. South to Canal will place you at the subway stop for the J, M, Z or the number 6 train. The 6 can also be picked up on Lafayette Street. A couple of blocks west to Broadway takes you to the M1 or M6 bus.

NEW YORK'S TOP TENS

★

TOP TEN
FANS' FAVORITE STARS

Madonna	1 West 64th Street
Barbra Streisand	320 Central Park West
Liza Minnelli	150 East 69th Street
Woody Allen	930 5th Avenue
Cher	14 East 4th Street
Bill Cosby	18 East 71st Street
Tom Cruise	14 East 4th Street
Richard Gere	26 East 10th Street
Diana Ross	781 5th Avenue
Frank Sinatra	100 East 50th Street

TOP 10 TEN
STAR-STUDDED BUILDINGS

Dakota	1 West 72nd Street
Trump Tower	721 5th Avenue
San Remo	145–146 Central Park West
The Langham	135 Central Park West
Waldorf-Astoria Towers	100 East 50th Street
Hotel des Artistes	1 West 67th Street
The Beresford	211 Central Park West
The Eldorado	300 Central Park West
American Thread Building	260 West Broadway
Silk Building	14 East 4th Street

T O P ★10 T E N

STARS' FAVORITE RESTAURANTS

Russian Tea Room	150 West 57th Street	265-0947
Le Cirque	58 East 65th Street	794-9292
Elaine's	1702 2nd Avenue	534-8103
Cafe Tabac	232 East 9th Street	674-7072
Tribeca Grill	375 Greenwich Street	941-3900
Carnegie Deli	857 7th Avenue	757-2245
Trattoria dell'Arte	900 7th Avenue	245-9800
The Four Seasons	99 East 52nd Street	754-9494
Rainbow Room	30 Rockefeller Plaza	632-5000
"21" Club	21 West 52nd Street	582-7200

T O P ★10 T E N

MOVIE LOCATIONS

Central Park	*Home Alone 2, The Prince of Tides, Marathon Man, Annie Hall, Still of the Night*
Plaza Hotel	*Big Business, Network, The Rose, Funny Girl, Plaza Suite, Home Alone 2, The Pickle, The Way We Were, North by Northwest, The Great Gatsby, Arthur, The Cotton Club, Crocodile Dundee*
Radio City Music Hall	*The Godfather, Radio Days, Annie Hall*
Empire State Building	*King Kong, On the Town, An Affair to Remember, Love Affair.*
Statue of Liberty	*Superman, Funny Girl, On the Town, Ghostbusters II*
Lincoln Center	*The Turning Point, Ghostbusters, Moonstruck, The Producers*
Russian Tea Room	*Manhattan, Tootsie, The Turning Point.*
The Dakota	*Rosemary's Baby, House of Strangers*
Grand Central Terminal	*The Prince of Tides, The Cotton Club, North by Northwest*
Café des Artistes	*The Money Pit, My Dinner with Andre*

T O P ⭐ T E N

STARS' FAVORITE BEAUTY SALONS

Elizabeth Arden 691 5th Avenue 832-3225
Clients include: **Lauren Bacall,**
Jacqueline Onassis,
Kathleen Turner,
Andie MacDowell

La Coupe 694 Madison Avenue 371-9230
Clients include: **Glenn Close,**
Carolyn Roehm,
Dustin Hoffman,
Mary Tyler Moore

Frederic Fekkai 754 5th Avenue 753-9500
Clients include: **Sigourney Weaver,**
Cindy Crawford,
Meryl Streep

Kenneth Beauty Salon Waldorf-Astoria 752-1800
Clients include: **Joan Rivers,**
Angie Dickinson

Georgette Klinger 501 Madison Avenue 848-3200
Clients include: **Liza Minnelli,**
James Woods

Il Makiage 107 East 60th Street 371-3992
Clients include: **Diana Ross,**
Raquel Welch,
Sly Stallone

Bruno Pittini 746 Madison Avenue 517-9660
Clients include: **Catherine Deneuve**
Eric Clapton

Pierre Michel Coiffeur Trump Tower 753-3995
Clients include: **Bernadette Peters,**
Lily Tomlin,
Tina Sinatra,
Margaux Heming-
way

Saks Fifth Avenue Salon 666 5th Avenue 940-4000
Clients include: **Sally Jessy Raphael**
Regis Philbin

Vidal Sassoon 767 5th Avenue 535-9200
Clients include: **Leslie Uggams,**
Cyndi Lauper,
Cher

T O P T E N

S T A R S'   F A V O R I T E   N I G H T   S P O T S

Tatou	151 East 50th Street	753-1144
"44"	Royalton Hotel (44 West 44th Street)	944-8844
Limelight	47 West 20th Street	807-7850
Palladium	126 East 14th Street	473-7171
Coffee Shop	29 Union Square West	243-7969
Au-Bar	41 East 58th Street	308-9455
Le Bar Bat	311 West 57th Street	307-7228
China Club	2130 Broadway	877-1166
Elaine's	1703 2nd Avenue	534-8103
Whiskey Bar	Paramount Hotel (235 West 46th Street)	819-0404

SEND YOUR REGARDS

★

Send a note of thanks, encouragement, or a simple hello to your favorite celebrity. The map below contains zip codes that divide up the city. Find the box that corresponds to the address of your particular star. Enclosing a stamped self-addressed envelope may spur a quicker, more positive response to your letter.

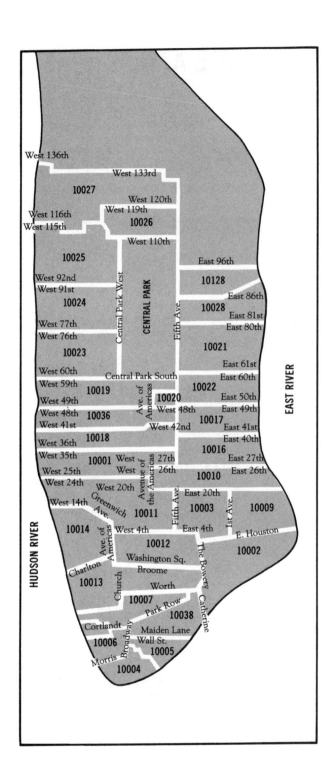

BIG APPLE ATTRACTIONS

ENTERTAINMENT TOURS

Backstage on Broadway Tours
228 West 47th Street
575-8065
*Lectures given backstage at various
Broadway theaters*

Carnegie Hall Tours
57th Street at 7th Avenue
247-7800

Lincoln Center Guided Tour
140 West 65th Street
877-1800

Metropolitan Opera House
140 West 65th Street
582-3512

NBC Studio Tour
30 Rockefeller Plaza
664-7174

New York City Opera
140 West 65th Street
870-5630
*Combines a performance with a
meal at an area restaurant*

Radio City Music Hall
Avenue of the Americas at 50th
Street
632-4041
Behind-the-scenes tour

FREE TELEVISION-SHOW TICKETS

"Attitudes"
Lifetime Television Network
Call 718-706-3537

"Donahue"
Send postcard to:
Donahue
NBC Tickets
30 Rockefeller Plaza
New York, NY 10102
Or call 664-6501

"Geraldo"
*Send stamped self-addressed,
envelope to:*
Geraldo Tickets
CBS Television
524 West 57th Street
New York, NY 10019
Or call 265-1283

"Gossip, Gossip, Gossip"
U.S.A. Network
Joan Rivers
254 West 57th Street
Call 975-5903

"Joan Rivers Show"
Call 975-5903

"Jane Whitney Show"
Untel Studios
841 9th Avenue
Call 957-1340

"David Letterman" Show
Send postcard to:
David Letterman Tickets
The Ed Sullivan Theater
1697 Broadway
New York, N.Y. 10019

**"Live with Regis and
Kathie Lee"**

Send postcard to:
Live Tickets
P.O. Box 777
Ansonia Station
New York, NY 10023–0777

For standby:
Be *at* 67 Columbus Avenue *at*
8:00 A.M.

"Maury Povich Show"
Send postcard to:
221 West 26th Street
New York, NY 10001
Or Call 989-3622

"Montel Williams Show"
Send Postcard to:
1481 Broadway
New York, NY 10036
Or call 840-1700

"The Richard Bey Show"
(WWOR, TV 9)
Call 201-392-8499

"Sally Jessy Raphael Show"
Send postcard to:
Sally Tickets
P.O. Box 1400
Radio City Station
New York, NY 10101
Or call 582-1722

"Saturday Night Live"
Send postcard to:
SNL Tickets
NBC Tickets
30 Rockefeller Plaza
New York, NY 10102

For standby:
Be *at* 30 Rockefeller Plaza *at* 9:00
A.M. *Saturday to receive tickets for
the* 11:30 P.M. *show that night*

Steampipe Alley
(WWOR, TV 9)
Call 201-330-2485

PERFORMANCE HALLS

Carnegie Hall	145 West 57th Street	247-7800
City Center	131 West 55th Street	246-8989
Joyce Theater	175 5th Avenue	242-0800
Lincoln Center	140 West 65th Street	307-7171
Alice Tully Hall		875-5050
Avery Fisher Hall		875-5030
Metropolitan Opera House		362-6000
New York State Theater		870-5700
Vivian Beaumont Theater		362-7600
Madison Square Garden	7th Avenue at 33rd Street	568-8300
Radio City Music Hall	Avenue of the Americas at 50th Street	757-3100

HALF-PRICE THEATER TICKETS

Lower Manhattan Theater Center
Two World Trade Center, mezzanine level
Monday–Saturday: 11:00 A.M.–5:30 P.M.
(Off-Broadway tickets sold 11:00 A.M.–1:00 P.M.

TKTS Booth
Duffy Square, 47th Street and Broadway
Open daily, 3:00 P.M.–8:00 P.M.
Music and Dance Booth
Bryant Park, 42nd Street and Avenue of the Americas
Tuesday, Thursday, Friday: Noon–2:00 P.M., 3:00 P.M.–7:00 P.M.
Wednesday–Saturday: 11:00 A.M.–2:00 P.M., 3:00 P.M.–7:00 P.M.
Sunday: Noon–6:00 P.M.

THEATERS

Ambassador	219 West 49th Street	239-6200
Belasco	111 West 44th Street	239-6200
Booth	222 West 45th Street	239-6200
Broadhurst	234 West 44th Street	239-6200
Broadway	Broadway at 53rd Street	239-6200
Brooks Atkinson	256 West 47th Street	719-4099
Circle in the Square	1633 Broadway	239-6200
Cort	138 West 48th Street	239-6200
Edison	240 West 47th Street	302-2302
Ethel Barrymore	243 West 47th Street	239-6200
Eugene O'Neill	230 West 49th Street	246-0220
Gershwin	51st Street off Broadway	586-6510
Helen Hayes	240 West 44th Street	944-9450
Imperial	249 West 45th Street	239-6200
John Golden	252 West 45th Street	239-6200
Longacre	220 West 48th Street	239-6200
Lunt-Fontanne	205 West 46th Street	575-9200
Lyceum	149 West 45th Street	239-6200
Majestic	247 West 44th Street	239-6200
Mark Hellinger	51st Street at Broadway	757-7064
Marquis	1535 Broadway	384-0100
Martin Beck	302 West 45th Street	246-6363
Minskoff	200 West 45th Street	869-0550
Music Box	239 West 45th Street	239-6200
Nederlander	208 West 41st Street	921-8000
Neil Simon	250 West 52nd Street	757-8646
Palace	1564 Broadway	757-2626
Plymouth	236 West 45th Street	239-6200
Royale	242 West 45th Street	239-6200
St. James	246 West 44th Street	398-0280
Shubert	225 West 44th Street	239-6200
Virginia	245 West 52nd Street	977-9370
Winter Garden	1634 Broadway	239-6200

VARIOUS POINTS OF INTEREST

Empire State Building
5th Avenue at 34th Street
Observation Deck: 736-3100

Jacob Javits Convention Center
11th Avenue
between 34th to 39th streets
216-2000

New York Stock Exchange
Wall and Broad Streets
695-2950

Rockefeller Center
5th Avenue at 50th Street
695-2950

St. Patrick's Cathedral
5th Avenue at 50th Street
753-2261

South Street Seaport
Fulton Street at Pier 16

United Nations
1st Avenue at 45th Street
963-7713

Visitors and Convention Bureau
2 Columbus Circle
397-7713

World Trade Center
Lower Manhattan
(can't miss the Twin Towers)
Observation Deck: 466-7377

MUSEUMS

**American Museum of
Natural History**
Central Park West at 79th Street
769-5100

**Ellis Island Immigration
Museum**
269-5775

Guggenheim Museum
5th Avenue at 89th Street
269-3500

Intrepid Sea-Air-Space Museum
Hudson River at 46th Street
245-0072

Jewish Museum
5th Avenue at 92nd Street
724-1143

Metropolitan Museum of Art
5th Avenue at 82nd Street
535-7710

Museum of Broadcasting
1 East 53rd Street
752-7684

Museum of Modern Art
11 West 53rd Street
708-9480

**Whitney Museum of
American Art**
Madison Avenue at 75th Street
570-3600

HAVE YOU HAD A

CELEBRITY SIGHTING?

Author Larry Wolfe Horwitz

Would Like to Hear From You

to Assist His Continuing Research.

You May Contact Him at

LARRY WOLFE PRODUCTIONS
1636 THIRD AVENUE, SUITE 354
NEW YORK, N.Y. 10128

INDEX